CHEROKEE MEDICINE MAN

Also by Robert J. Conley

The Witch of Goingsnake and Other Stories (Norman, 1988)
Ned Christie's War (New York, 1990)
Mountain Windsong: A Novel of the Trail of Tears (Norman, 1992)
Nickajack (New York, 1992)
War Woman: A Novel of the Real People (New York, 1997)
Brass (New York, 1999)
Cherokee Dragon: A Novel of the Real People (New York, 2000)
Medicine War (New York, 2001)
Sequoyah (New York, 2002)
(with David G. Fitzgerald) *Cherokee* (Portland, 2002)

Cherokee Medicine Man

THE LIFE AND WORK
OF A MODERN-DAY HEALER

ROBERT J. CONLEY

UNIVERSITY OF OKLAHOMA PRESS : NORMAN

Publication of this book is made possible through the generosity of Edith Kinney Gaylord.

Library of Congress Cataloging-in-Publication Data

Conley, Robert J.
    Cherokee medicine man : the life and work of a modern-day
    healer / Robert J. Conley.
        p.   cm.
    ISBN 0–8061–3665–0 (alk. paper)
    1. Little Bear, John.   2. Cherokee Indians—Biography.
    3. Shamans—Biography.   4. Cherokee Indians—Religion.
    5. Cherokee Indians—Rites and ceremonies.   I. Title.

E99.C5L54 2005
299.7'8557'0092—dc22
[B]

                                                        2004058036

2 3 4 5 6 7 8 9 10

Contents

CONTENTS

CHEROKEE MEDICINE MAN

Introduction

I thought everything was just fine with me. I was writing well, had contracts lined up, was feeling good at sixty years old. I could afford to keep myself in Wild Turkey and have a few drinks each night before going to bed. I was waking up at six the next morning feeling fine. Everything was all right. Then, within a matter of two days, two different people came to see me, each with the same message. "Little Bear says you need to come and see him." They were talking about John Little Bear, Cherokee medicine man. I had been to see Little Bear many times in the past, but I had not been to see him for quite a while. I didn't think I needed to see him. But when Little Bear tells me that I should do something, I take him seriously, so I went up to his house on the hill the next Sunday.

It was one of those Sundays when Little Bear has sweats scheduled, and on those days people from all over the place show up, lots of people, all kinds of people—Cherokees, Creeks, white people, black people, Mexicans. They come from all around the Cherokee country of northeast Oklahoma, and they come from outside: Oklahoma City; Dallas, Texas; Fort Smith, Arkansas; other places as well. So I went prepared to sweat, and I waited my turn. Finally, Little Bear's assistant, Frank, motioned to me. I followed him with the others out to the sweat lodge. It was a cold day in February.

Delaying as long as possible, I at last stripped off to a pair of cutoff jeans, and when Frank called us into the lodge, I went in and took my place. Frank dipped the medicine (water in which certain herbs have been boiled) out of the bucket with a gourd dipper and poured it over the hot rocks. Almost instantly, the lodge was filled with hot steam. I did all right in there, but I experienced chills, and I actually shivered there in the incredible heat. At the same time, I was sweating profusely.

Following the sweat, I went back to the house to wait for Little Bear. It was getting into evening by then, and I had been there since about one o'clock in the afternoon. Little Bear's wife passed by me once and said, "Little Bear's waiting till everyone else is done, so he can have you by yourself." At last he called me, and I went back to his room where he was waiting.

"Mr. Conley," he said, "you're drinking way too much. I been watching you. I want you to cut way back. I seen your liver, and it has a white line around it."

"Little Bear," I said, "I trust you, and when you tell me something, I believe you, but it's weird to think about you watching me at my house."

He laughed, and then he told me that he watches everyone he makes medicine for. I told him I would follow his advice. At home later, I told my wife, Evelyn, what had transpired. I went into my bar and looked wistfully at the nearly full bottle of Wild Turkey there. I had enjoyed only one evening out of it. I left it alone. Two nights later, I still had not touched the bottle. I was sitting with a cup of coffee watching television when I saw a shadow move across the window outside in the darkness.

"Little Bear," I shouted, "is that you? Goddamn it, I'm drinking coffee."

Perhaps a half hour later, Evelyn came home from our daughter's house. She said that a big bird had flown right in front of her. She thought it was an owl.

"Hell," I said, "it was Little Bear."

I was grumbling over my new situation. It did not enter my mind to ignore Little Bear's advice, but that did not mean I had to like it. At sixty years old, I did not need another mother, I told myself. Then I asked myself, just how did I get into this situation in the first place? How did it come about that I have a medicine man watching over me, sending for me instead of waiting until I go see him with some kind of complaint? I've been thinking about that for a couple of weeks now, two weeks in which I have not touched the Wild Turkey bottle in my bar, and perhaps I can begin to answer the question by going back to when I first met Little Bear.

I like to say that I met Little Bear in jail. That's not even quite a half-truth though. I actually first met him in a building in Tulsa, Oklahoma, owned by the Tulsa Police Department. I don't know what it's used for normally, but the Tulsa police had given Clu Gulager permission to use it for a get-together for his film crew. Clu, a Cherokee film actor, had moved back to Oklahoma from Los Angeles with the intention of producing a film locally. Clu and I had become acquainted some years earlier, and he had asked me if I would like to appear in his film. I had agreed.

I went to Tulsa for the meeting Clu had called, and Little Bear was one of the other actors there. During a break, we went outside to smoke, and we got pretty well acquainted with one another. I discovered that Little Bear was quite a linguist, speaking not just English and Cherokee but also Creek and Choctaw. I recognized his family name, because his grandmother was a well-known Cherokee medicine woman in the area. I had never met her, but I had certainly heard of her. She was known far and wide, and for good reason.

I saw Little Bear next on the day of the actual filming. Clu had gotten permission to shoot a scene in the jail. They had cleaned out one cell for us and loaned us some inmate clothing. Little Bear and I and some other actors were playing prisoners. Clu had asked me to shave my mustache and my head, and he was contrasting me in the picture with Little Bear, who was wearing a full beard at the time. He shot some scenes of the two of us with our heads together talking in hushed tones. We spent a long day in that jail cell and wound up on the cutting room floor.

Over the next several weeks, maybe months, I saw Little Bear occasionally in Tahlequah, Oklahoma, usually in a parking lot somewhere. He would drive into town with his wife, park the van, and wait in it while she went inside some store to do some shopping. We would chat for a few minutes there at his van, talking about our jailhouse episode or asking one another for any news from Clu. Clu had gone back to Los Angeles by then. Little Bear and I were casual acquaintances with a shared experience and a common friend who happened to be a celebrity.

Then sometime later, I was going through some hard times, not an unusual situation for a writer to be in. Contracts were slow, and checks were even slower. I had received some awards, and I was being asked fairly often to make appearances at college campuses and bookstores from Los Angeles to Cherokee, North Carolina, but things just weren't quite right. I couldn't put a finger on it, but I felt at loose ends.

I had driven to the supermarket in Tahlequah to do some shopping. I parked the car and was walking across the parking lot when I heard someone call my name. I looked around to see Little Bear sitting in his van. I walked over to say hello, and we chatted for a bit. Then Little Bear said to me, "I've started practicing. You ought to come and see me sometime." I said, "Oh. Okay," sort of casually, and went on my way. Later at home, I told Evelyn what Little Bear had said.

"When someone like that tells you to come and see him," she said to me, "you'd better do it."

I did.

Little Bear's house sits on top of Stick Ross Mountain just outside of Tahlequah. It's on a turn off the main road onto a dirt road. His grandmother's house is located just where the dirt road meets the paved road, and the next turn is the drive up to Little Bear's house. It's rural, quiet, and peaceful. I found Little Bear at home, and we sat in his living room, smoking cigarettes and drinking coffee.

"Mr. Conley," he said, "the reason I hollered at you the other day is that I seen you walking across that parking lot, and there was part of you walking along ten feet behind you."

I was amazed. He had expressed exactly the way I had been feeling, although I would never have been able to put it in those words. I told him what had been going on in my life, and he sent me out to buy some nonfilter cigarettes and bring them back to him. I did that, and he sent me away again to give him time to work with the cigarettes, to put the medicine in them. When I returned again, he told me how to use them. I followed his instructions, and things did get better. After that, I went to see Little Bear often, and I began going to the Sunday sweats. One day while we were talking casually, Little Bear told me that he wanted me to write a book about him and about the medicine, to let people know "what Indian medicine is really about." He told some of the people who came to him with their problems to talk to me freely, assuring them that their names would not be used. I agreed, and I started taking notes, but I did not have a handle on the shape or form of the book. Things stayed that way for a time, and then I got the messages that Little Bear wanted to see me, and I got his advice about my drinking.

In the pages that follow, I'll introduce Little Bear and let him tell his story and the story of the medicine. In addition, I'll present some of the tales that were told to me by others, people who came to Little Bear for help. You'll learn what their problems were, why they went to Little Bear with those problems, and how he helped them. In short, you'll find out just what Little Bear, Cherokee medicine man, does "for the people." What you will not find here are recipes, formulae, or how-to instructions of any kind. Those are secret. They are only for the trained medicine person, and dabbling in Indian medicine can be a very dangerous thing to do. This book is intended only to give the reader a basic understanding of the nature and purpose of Indian medicine. That is all. In order to understand the story of Little Bear, it is necessary first to take a step backward and examine the culture and myths of the Cherokee people and the history of Cherokee medicine.

1

A Brief History of the Cherokees and the Origins of Medicine

There are different stories and theories about where the Cherokees came from originally, but when they were first encountered by Europeans, they were living in approximately 250 autonomous towns scattered over parts of what are now the states of North and South Carolina, Tennessee, Kentucky, Virginia, West Virginia, Alabama, and Georgia. They called themselves Ani-yunwiya (the Real People, Principal People, or Original People) or Ani-Kituwagi, the People of Keetoowah, or Keetoowah People. Keetoowah is said to be the Mother Town, or the original town, of the Cherokee people. All other Cherokee towns grew out of Keetoowah. They spoke an Iroquoian language, related to Mohawk, Seneca, Onondaga, Oneida, Cayuga, and others. These other Iroquoian people lived north, in what is now New York and around the Great Lakes. The Cherokees were surrounded with mostly Muskogean-speaking peoples. There were also a few Siouan-speaking tribes in the general area.

Cherokee families were matrilineal clans, meaning that descent was traced strictly through the female line. Children belonged to their mothers and to their mothers' clans. Women owned the homes and gardens, and when a man married, he went to live in his wife's house. Europeans had a hard time understanding the Cherokee families, early on making comments like, "The Cherokees have a petticoat government," and "Among the Cherokees, the woman rules the roost." One wit wrote, "A Cherokee woman will get a stick and beat her husband from his head to his heels, and when he can stand it no more, he'll turn over and let her beat the other side."

Cherokees lived in autonomous towns, having no central government. Each town had its own two chiefs, a war chief and a peace chief, and each chief had his council of advisers. It is not known precisely how the chiefs became chiefs. They did not have absolute or coercive power. They led by persuasion, and they could be removed from office. Perhaps they had a system similar to the Northern Iroquois, where the clan women selected the chiefs, and the clan women could recall them. That's speculation.

Cherokees believed in a world of three parts: the world we live on, which is an island floating on water; the world above, a great "Sky Vault" covering all and where all the original life-forms lived; and the world below, a chaotic world populated by all kinds of monsters who can often find their way to the world we live on through the waterways. The great task of the people was to maintain balance and harmony on this earth, caught between the two powerful and opposed otherworlds. This was done through ritual and ceremony, often appealing to the many spirits that surround us. Into this delicate and precarious world came the Europeans.

The first Europeans to venture into Cherokee lands were the Spaniards following Hernando de Soto on his brutal expedition of 1540. They seem not to have bothered the Cherokees much; however, they did enough damage elsewhere that the Cherokees were certainly aware of it. The Cherokees seem then to have been left alone for about a hundred years before the first Englishmen visited, seeking trade relations. From then on, Cherokee history is much involved with that of the British colonies in North America and later, of course, with the United States.

The English soon tired of having to deal with each Cherokee town separately, and they managed to convince the Cherokees to appoint a sort-of trade commissioner. The man's name was recorded as "Wrosetasetoe," a name that no Cherokee can translate. It was apparently a poor British attempt at spelling a Cherokee name. When Wrosetasetoe died, he was replaced by Amaedohi, whom the English called "Moytoy." They also called him the "emperor" of the Cherokees. Surely the Cherokees thought of him as nothing more than a trade commissioner; however, the position would slowly evolve into that of an elected principal chief.

Somewhere along the way, due to the widespread use of the Mobilian jargon, a trade language used by almost everyone in the region, the Cherokees accepted the name "Chalakee" from the jargon and began using it themselves in the form of "Tsalagi." In English it became "Cherokee."

The Cherokee relationship with the British colonies was an unstable one. The Cherokees were often at war with one or more of the colonies, often allied with one or more of them. At the end of each war, the English would ask for a little Cherokee land with the treaty. Things were often complicated by intrigues between the English, Spanish, and French. But by the time of the American Revolution, one Cherokee had seen enough land loss. He decided to draw the line. His name was Tsiyu-gansini, Dragging Canoe. Because of trade and intermarriage with the traders, the Cherokee lifestyle had already altered dramatically. Old skills were abandoned and lost because of trade goods, and the European-style family was slowing taking hold in place of the old clan system.

Dragging Canoe meant to retain what he could of the old ways and to put a stop to the loss of Cherokee land. He found that his best ally in this effort was England. The king of England had passed a proclamation declaring that no one could buy or trade for Indian land but the king. He meant to contain his colonies along the East Coast. If he could be successful in that effort, the colonists would not be moving farther west onto Cherokee lands.

About the time Dragging Canoe came into prominence, the American Revolution broke out, and Dragging Canoe became a British ally in the war against the new Americans. Not all Cherokees agreed with him though, and so the Cherokees were split. When Dragging Canoe's towns were burned by the Americans, he moved to a new location on Chickamauga Creek, and he and his followers became known as Chickamaugas or Chickamauga Cherokees. They soon became a mixed group of full-blood Cherokees, mixed-blood Cherokees, white Loyalists or Tories, Creeks, and Shawnees. (The young Tecumseh was with them for a time.) At the end of the Revolution, the British ceased supplying them with arms, but Dragging Canoe continued the fight. When Dragging Canoe died in 1791, the Chickamauga movement slowly fell apart, and in 1792 the Cherokees' war with the Americans was over.

One group of Chickamaugas moved west that same year, settling for a time in Missouri, but following the great earthquake of 1811, they moved farther west and south to settle in what is now western Arkansas. They became known as the Western Cherokee Nation, and the U.S. government dealt with them as a separate nation from the Cherokee Nation. In Arkansas, they became embroiled in a long and bitter war with the Osages.

Back in the old Cherokee country, pressures for Cherokee removal had begun, and they intensified. As early as 1803, President Thomas Jefferson had signed a compact with the state of Georgia promising to remove all Indians from Georgia as soon as possible. Georgia was getting impatient. Other southern states joined in, and when Andrew Jackson was elected president, they gained a strong ally. Jackson managed to push through his Indian Removal Bill in 1830, and it became law by only one vote. The other southern Indian tribes began to move, but the Cherokee Nation, under the leadership of their popularly elected principal chief, John Ross, resisted, taking their case all the way to the U.S. Supreme Court, where they won.

But Cherokee jubilation over the victory did not last long, for they soon discovered that Jackson refused to acknowledge the Court's decision, saying, "Justice Marshall has made his decision. Now let him enforce it." Disheartened, some Cherokees signed a treaty of total removal, called the Treaty of New Echota, on December 29, 1835. The treaty was fraudulent, having been signed by men who were not elected to any Cherokee Nation governmental positions, but nevertheless it was ratified by the U.S. Senate and enforced by the president. The majority of Cherokees still resisted for a time, but beginning in 1838, the U.S. Army began to forcibly remove them from their homes. They were placed in stockade prisons, where many sickened and died. When the roundup was nearly complete, the army began to move them west over what became known as the Trail of Tears.

Twenty thousand Cherokees were moved in thirteen waves, the entire process taking several months to complete. It has been estimated that one-fourth of the Cherokee population of the time lies buried beside the trail in unmarked graves. It has also been said that there was not a single Cherokee family that did not lose someone during the removal. A small group of Cherokees managed to remain behind in the mountains of North Carolina. They were eventually able to purchase land and stay, and their descendants are today the Eastern Band of Cherokee Indians.

The rest, the majority, those who survived the trail, moved into what is now northeast Oklahoma. It was then the Cherokee Nation. The people of the Western Cherokee Nation were moved across the line from Arkansas to join them, and the Western Cherokee Nation ceased to exist. Embittered from their ordeal, some of the people who had suffered the Trail of Tears began to assassinate the people who had signed the Removal Treaty. There was retaliation, and a civil war nearly developed in the Cherokee Nation. After much violence, an uneasy peace was restored, and the Cherokee Nation entered into what has been called by some historians its Golden Age.

Cities were laid out. Schools and churches were built. A newspaper was published in English and Cherokee, making use of the symbols that Sequoyah had presented to the Cherokee people back in 1828. But the Golden Age lasted not quite twenty years.

When the Civil War broke out in the United States, the Cherokees were almost immediately embroiled in it. Stand Watie, whose brother had been killed for signing the Removal Treaty, raised a regiment of Cherokees for the Confederacy. And though Principal Chief John Ross wanted to keep the Cherokee Nation neutral, he was eventually forced to sign a treaty with the Confederate states. Many Cherokees did not want to fight for the South and joined the pro-union "Pin" Indians. The Civil War raged in the Cherokee Nation. John Ross later repudiated his Confederate treaty, and Stand Watie declared a Confederate Cherokee Nation, with himself not only as general of the army but also principal chief. He was the last Confederate general to surrender.

Cherokee involvement in the Civil War provided the U.S. government the excuse it needed to impose yet another treaty on the

Cherokee Nation (and the other four of the so-called Five Civilized Tribes). The new treaty stripped the Cherokee Nation of many of the powers of government and organized the five tribes into Indian Territory, a first step toward statehood. The Cherokee Nation, almost destroyed during the Civil War and its government seriously fractured by the new treaty, began again to rebuild. And it made tremendous strides. Once again, it built schools, creating the first free, compulsory public school system in the country, perhaps in the world. (Education was the highest single line item on the Cherokee Nation's budget.) It built male and female seminaries, the first institutions of higher education west of the Mississippi River. A two-story, brick capitol was built in Tahlequah. The Cherokee Nation had a national prison, a national orphanage, an insane asylum, and a supreme court building. (The orphanage and the insane asylum were necessary because of the Civil War.) It had a "School for the Colored." A Cherokee installed the first telephone west of the Mississippi River, running the line from the Cherokee capitol in Tahlequah to the offices of the Bureau of Indian Affairs in Muskogee. By 1907, the Cherokee Nation had produced more college graduates than the states of Arkansas and Texas combined.

But powerful forces were at work to abolish the Cherokee Nation and create the state of Oklahoma. One of their main arguments was that the Cherokee Nation could not maintain law and order within its own borders. The whole of Indian Territory was in fact a lawless land, harboring fugitives of every stripe, and it was that way precisely because the United States had forbidden the Cherokee Nation and the other four tribes to arrest or try anyone other than one of their own tribal citizens. The United States had created an impossible situation for the tribal governments to deal with.

Eventually, the forces for statehood prevailed. The lands of the Cherokee Nation were allotted to individuals, the surplus being made available to white settlers. The property of the Cherokee Nation was taken over by the new state or sold to individuals. The Cherokee Nation was all but destroyed, with the president of the United States appointing a Cherokee chief when he needed land transfer documents signed. The chiefs of this period became known as the "Chiefs for a Day."

During this time, under a federal law enacted during the 1930s, a group of full-blood Cherokees formed the United Keetoowah Band of Cherokee Indians in Oklahoma. They applied for and received a federal charter and incorporation and received, under the law, "all the rights and privileges of any federally recognized Indian tribe." Then in 1983, ignoring the existence of the Keetoowah Band, President Ronald Reagan returned elections to the Cherokee Nation. To this day, there are two federally recognized Cherokee tribes, both headquartered in Tahlequah. (The Eastern Band in North Carolina is a third.) Both the Cherokee Nation and the Keetoowah Band are growing, operating federal programs and tribal enterprises, and there is an often not too subtle "cold war" taking place between the two.

Cherokees today come in all kinds of manifestations. The tribal population of the Cherokee Nation is in excess of 200,000, but of that number, perhaps 8,000 are full-blood or nearly so. The Cherokee Nation will accept for membership anyone who is a direct descendant of anyone listed on the Dawes Commission roll, which was drawn up in preparation for Oklahoma statehood. Many of its members have infinitesimal amounts of Cherokee blood. The Keetoowah Band, on the other hand, enrolls only people who have one-quarter or more Cherokee blood. There are about 8,000 members of the Keetoowah Band.

Amazingly, throughout all of the Cherokee Nation's turbulent history, there have remained people who cling to ancient traditions, and one of those traditions is the medicine. The subject of this book, John Little Bear, is a traditional practitioner of that medicine. Before getting to his story, it might be well to consider the history of that medicine, for it has a story and a life of its own.

The following story from the Cherokee oral tradition was collected by ethnologist James Mooney on the reservation of the Eastern Band of Cherokee Indians in North Carolina and published in *Myths of the Cherokee* in the 19th Annual Report of the Bureau of American Ethnology in 1897–98. The stories from Mooney reprinted here appear just as Mooney presented them, together with his often peculiar punctuation and occasionally peculiar spelling. The only change is that I have not used the diacritical marks that he used over Cherokee vowels in his spelling of Cherokee words.

ORIGIN OF DISEASE AND MEDICINE

In the old days the beasts, birds, fishes, insects and plants could all talk, and they and the people lived together in peace and friendship. But as time went on the people increased so rapidly that their settlements spread over the whole earth, and the poor animals found themselves beginning to be cramped for room. This was bad enough, but to make it worse Man invented bows, knives, blowguns, spears, and hooks, and began to slaughter the larger animals, birds, and fishes for their flesh or their skins, while the smaller creatures, such as the frogs and worms, were crushed and trodden upon without thought, out of pure carelessness or contempt. So the animals resolved to consult upon measures for their common safety.

The Bears were the first to meet in council in their townhouse under Kuwahi mountain, the "Mulberry Place," and the old White Bear chief presided. After each in turn had complained of the way in which Man killed their friends, ate their flesh, and used their skins for his own purposes, it was decided to begin war at once against him. Some one asked what weapons Man used to destroy them. "Bows and arrows, of course," cried all the Bears in chorus. "And what are they made of?" was the next question. "The bow of wood, and the string of our entrails," replied one of the Bears. It was then proposed that they make a bow and some arrows and see if they could not use the same weapons against Man himself. So one Bear got a nice piece of locust wood and another sacrificed himself for the good of the rest in order to furnish a piece of his entrails for the string. But when everything was ready and the first Bear stepped up to make the trial, it was found that in letting the arrow fly after drawing back the bow, his long claws caught the string and spoiled the shot. This was annoying, but someone suggested that they might trim his claws, which was accordingly done, and on a second trial it was found that the arrow went straight to the mark. But here the chief, the old White Bear, objected, saying it was necessary that they should have long claws in order to be able to climb trees. "One of us has already died to furnish the bow string, and if we now cut off our claws we must all starve together. It is better to trust to the teeth and claws that nature gave us, for it is plain that man's weapons were not intended for us."

No one could think of any better plan, so the old chief dismissed the council and the Bears dispersed to the woods and thickets without having concerted any way to prevent the increase of the human race. Had the results of the council been otherwise, we should now be at war with the Bears, but as it is, the hunter does not even ask the Bear's pardon when he kills one.

The Deer next held a council under their chief, the Little Deer, and after some talk decided to send rheumatism to every hunter who should kill one of them unless he took care to ask their pardon for the offense. They sent notice of their decision to the nearest settlement of Indians and told them at the same time what to do when necessity forced them to kill one of the Deer tribe. Now, whenever a hunter shoots a Deer, the Little Deer, who is swift as the wind and cannot be wounded, runs quickly up to the spot and, bending over the blood-stains, asks the spirit of the Deer if it has heard the prayer of the hunter for pardon. If the reply be "Yes," all is well, and the Little Deer goes on his way; but if the reply be "No," he follows on the trail of the hunter, guided by the drops of blood on the ground, until he arrives at his cabin in the settlement, when the Little Deer enters invisibly and strikes the hunter with rheumatism, so that he becomes at once a helpless cripple. No hunter who has regard for his health ever fails to ask pardon of the Deer for killing it, although some hunters who have not learned the prayer may try to turn aside the Little Deer from his pursuit by building a fire behind them in the trail.

Next came the Fishes and Reptiles, who had their own complaints against Man. They held their council together and determined to make their victims dream of snakes twining about them in slimy folds and blowing foul breath in their faces, or to make them dream of eating raw or decaying fish, so that they would lose appetite, sicken and die. This is why people dream about snakes and fish.

Finally the Birds, Insects, and smaller animals came together for the same purpose, and the Grubworm was chief of the council. It was decided that each in turn should give an opinion, and then they would vote on the question as to whether or not Man was guilty. Seven votes should be enough to condemn him. One after another denounced Man's cruelty and injustice toward the other animals and voted in favor of his death. The Frog spoke first, saying: "We must do something to check the increase of the race, or people will become so numerous that we shall be crowded from off the earth. See how they have kicked me about because I'm ugly, as they say, until my back is covered with sores;" and here he showed the spots on his skin. Next came the Bird—no one remembers now which one it was—who condemned Man "because he burns my feet off," meaning the way in which the hunter barbecues birds by impaling them on a stick set over the fire, so that their feathers and tender feet are singed off. Others followed in the same strain. The Ground-squirrel alone ventured to say a good word for Man, who seldom hurt him because he was so small, but this made the others so angry that they fell upon the Ground-squirrel and tore him with their claws, and the stripes are on his back to this day.

They began then to devise and name so many new diseases, one after another, that had not their invention at last failed them, no one of the human race would have been able to survive. The Grubworm grew constantly more pleased as the name of each disease was called off, until at last they reached the end of the list, when someone proposed to make menstruation sometimes fatal to women. On this he rose up in his place and cried: "Wado! [Thanks!] I'm glad some more of them will die, for they are getting so thick that they tread on me." The thought fairly made him shake with joy, so that he fell over backward and could not get on his feet again, but had to wriggle off on his back, as the Grubworm has done ever since.

When the plants, who were friendly to Man, heard what had been done by the animals, they determined to defeat the latters' evil designs. Each Tree, Shrub, and Herb, down even to the Grasses and Mosses, agreed to furnish a cure for some one of the diseases named, and each said: "I shall appear to help Man when he calls upon me in his need." Thus came medicine; and the plants, every one of which has its use if we only knew it, furnish the remedy to counteract the evil wrought by the revengeful animals. Even weeds were made for some good purpose, which we must find out for ourselves. When the doctor does not know what medicine to use for a sick man the spirit of the plant tells him.

Much could be written about the medicines alluded to in this tale. In fact, much has already been written about it. Mooney himself, in *Sacred Formulas of the Cherokees* (7th Annual Report, Bureau of American Ethnology), covered a great deal of this type of material. Charles Hudson, in his fine work, *The Southeastern Indians,* dealt with much of it. Virgil J. Vogel dealt with the topic admirably for American Indians in general in his monumental work, *American Indian Medicine.* There are many more such studies.

But much Cherokee medicine deals with another kind of illness from a darker source. Many ailments are attributed by Cherokees to the dealings of jealous or disgruntled people with makers of bad medicine. These people will go to a practitioner with no scruples or conscience to pay for medicine to cause someone else to suffer. The suffering thus brought about may be financial, or it may be physical, mental, or all of these. It can even go so far as to cause death. Once this process has been set in motion, there is no hope for the victim other than to seek the services of another doctor, one who can not only determine the cause of the ailment but can also provide a cure for it.

The subject of this book, John Little Bear, told me the following tale. A long time ago, he said, Indians all had medicine for fighting wars with their enemies. Some was to make them stronger, to make them invisible to their enemies, to make their arrows fly straighter, and so on. Each tribe had its medicine people, and if they should get into a fight with one another, it would be not only a physical war but also a medicine war. As time went by, some people began to ask themselves, "What would happen if I were to use some of this war medicine against such and such a family?" When they tried it, all kinds of bad things started happening to the unfortunate family. From there it went to just one person. Perhaps someone had a grudge against someone else or was jealous of someone else, and he or she tried to use the war medicine or some variation of it on that person.

Some of the war medicine was intended to confuse the enemy. Perhaps medicine would be buried in two different places facing two different directions. The enemy would become confused not knowing which way to turn. Now that same medicine is used on a family to confuse them and break them up. There is medicine for trading horses—or cars. There is medicine for borrowing money from a bank, for help in getting a job, for creating harmony so everyone will get along well together, and there is medicine for creating disharmony to break up friendships or families.

Medicine people will work around the clock making strong medicine for any or all of these purposes, mixing the herbs, brewing the drink or preparing the tobacco, putting the sacred songs into the medicine. But now, according to Little Bear, when the old medicine people pass on, leaving their medicine books behind, there are many younger people who will take those books and decide to experiment with the magical formulae they find in them. They lack the feelings, the convictions, and the controls of the older generation. They just want to try it out and see if it will work against someone they may have a grudge against. This is evil. It is a very dangerous thing to have going on.

Because of that, many of the older medicine people will pass their books along to another medicine person, one that they trust. Several are bringing their books to Little Bear rather than leave them for their children to get hold of. Among the older generation, two medicine men will likely get together to share their secrets. Each will learn from the other. When one passes on, the other will inherit his books and all of his secrets. Little Bear has such a partner, a man perhaps ten or fifteen years older than he is, who will be leaving him his books. According to Little Bear, there are songs in his own books that can kill someone in a matter of days. He does not use these songs, but he does know them.

From where did all of this kind of medicine originate? It is not much talked about, and there is very little in the recorded material. There are some hints in the tales collected by Mooney. Here is one from *Myths of the Cherokee*. A few others will follow.

THE WOLF'S REVENGE

Kanati had wolves to hunt for him, because they are good hunters and never fail. He once sent out two wolves at once. One went to the east and did not return. The other went to the north, and when he returned at night and did not find his fellow he knew he must be in trouble and started after him. After traveling on some time he found his brother lying nearly dead beside a great green snake (salikwa yi) which had attacked him. The snake itself was too badly wounded to crawl away, and the angry wolf, who had magic powers, taking out several hairs from his own whiskers, shot them into the body of the snake and killed it. He then hurried back to Kanati, who sent the Terrapin after a great doctor who lived in the west to save the wounded wolf. The wolf went back to help his brother and by his magic powers, he had him cured long before the doctor came from the west, because the Terrapin was such a slow traveler and the doctor had to prepare his roots before he started.

THE UKTENA AND THE ULUNSU TI

Long ago—hilahi yu—when the Sun became angry at the people on earth and sent a sickness to destroy them, the Little Men changed a man into a monster snake, which they called Uktena, "The Keen-eyed," and sent him to kill her. He failed to do the work, and the Rattlesnake had to be sent instead, which made the Uktena so jealous and angry that the people were afraid of him and had him taken up to Galun lati to stay with the other dangerous things. He left others behind him, though, nearly as large and dangerous as himself, and they hide now in deep pools in the river and about lonely passes in the high mountains, the places which the Cherokees call "Where the Uktena stays."

Those who know say that the Uktena is a great snake, as large around as a tree trunk, with horns on its head, and a bright, blazing crest like a diamond upon its forehead, and scales glittering like sparks of fire. It has rings or spots of color along its whole length, and cannot be wounded except by shooting in the seventh spot from the head, because under this spot are its heart and its life. The blazing diamond is called Ulunsu ti, "Transparent," and he who can win it may become the greatest wonder worker of the tribe, but it is worth a man's life to attempt it, for whoever is seen by the Uktena is so dazed by the bright light that he runs toward the snake instead of trying to escape. Even to see the Uktena asleep is death, not to the hunter himself, but to his family.

Of all the daring warriors who have started out in search of the Ulunsu ti only Agan-uni tsi ever came back successful. The East Cherokees still keep the one he brought. It is like a large transparent crystal, nearly the shape of a cartridge bullet, with a blood-red streak running through the center from top to bottom. The owner keeps it wrapped in a whole deer skin, inside an earthen jar hidden away in a secret cave in the mountains. Every seven days he feeds it with the blood of small game, rubbing the blood all over the crystal as soon as the animal has been killed. Twice a year it must have the blood of a deer or some other large animal. Should he forget to feed it at the proper time it would come out from its cave at night in a shape of fire and fly through the air to slake its thirst with the lifeblood of the conjurer or some one of his people. He may save himself from this danger by telling it, when he puts it away, that he will not need it again for a long time. It will then go quietly to sleep and feel no hunger until it is again brought out to be consulted. Then it must be fed again with blood before it is used.

No white man must ever see it and no person but the owner will venture near it for fear of sudden death. Even the conjurer who keeps it is afraid of it, and changes its hiding place every once in a while so that it cannot learn the way out. When he dies it will be buried with him. Otherwise it will come out of its cave, like a blazing star, to search for his grave, night after night for seven years, when, if still not able to find him, it will go back to sleep forever where he has placed it.

Whoever owns the Ulunsu ti is sure of success in hunting, love, rainmaking, and every other business, but its great use is in life prophecy. When it is consulted for this purpose the future is seen mirrored in the clear crystal as a tree is reflected in the quiet stream below, and the conjurer knows whether the sick man will recover, whether the warrior will return from battle, or whether the youth will live to be old.

THE RED MAN AND THE UKTENA

Two brothers were hunting together, and when they came to a good camping place in the mountains they made a fire, and while one gathered bark to put up a shelter the other started up the creek to look for a deer. Soon he heard a noise on the top of the ridge as if two animals were fighting. He hurried through the bushes to see what it might be, and when he came to the spot he found a great uktena coiled around a man and choking him to death. The man was fighting for his life, and called out to the hunter: "Help me, nephew; he is your enemy as well as mine." The hunter took good aim, and, drawing the arrow to the head, sent it through the body of the uktena, so that the blood spouted from the hole. The snake loosed its coils with a snapping noise, and went tumbling down the ridge into the valley, tearing up the earth like a water spout as it rolled.

The stranger stood up, and it was the Asga ya Gi gagei, the Red Man of the Lightning. He said to the hunter: "You have helped me, and now I will reward you, and give you a medicine so that you can always find game." They waited until it was dark, and then went down the ridge to where the dead uktena had rolled, but by this time the birds and insects had eaten the body and only the bones were left. In one place were flashes of light coming up from the ground, and on digging here, just under the surface, the Red Man found a scale of the uktena. Next he went over to a tree that had been struck by lightning, and gathering a handful of splinters he made a fire and burned the uktena scale to a coal. He wrapped this in a piece of deerskin and gave it to the hunter, saying: "As long as you keep this you can always kill game." Then he told the hunter that when he went back to camp he must hang up the medicine on a tree outside, because it was very strong and dangerous. He told him also that when he went into the cabin he would find his brother lying inside nearly dead on account of the presence of the uktena's scale, but he must take a small piece of cane, which the Red Man gave him, and scrape a little of it into water and give it to his brother to drink and he would be well again. Then the Red Man was gone, and the hunter could not see where he went. He returned to camp alone, and found his brother very sick, but soon cured him with the medicine from the cane, and that day and the next, and every day after, he found game whenever he went for it.

NUN YUNU WI, THE STONE MAN

This is what the old men told me when I was boy.

Once when all the people of the settlement were out in the mountains on a great hunt one man who had gone on ahead climbed to the top of a high ridge and found a large river on the other side. While he was looking across he saw an old man walking about on the opposite ridge, with a cane that seemed to be made of some bright, shining rock. The hunter watched and saw that every little while the old man would point his cane in a certain direction, then draw it back and smell the end of it. At last he pointed it in the direction of the hunting camp on the other side of the mountain, and this time when he drew back the staff he sniffed it several times as if it smelled very good, and then started along the ridge straight for the camp. He moved very slowly, with the help of the cane, until he reached the end of the ridge, when he threw the cane out into the air and it became a bridge of shining rock stretching across the river. After he had crossed over upon the bridge it became a cane again, and the old man picked it up and started over the mountain toward the camp.

The hunter was frightened, and felt sure that it meant mischief, so he hurried on down the mountain and took the shortest trail back to the camp to get there before the old man. When he got there and told his story the medicine-man said the old man was a wicked cannibal monster called Nun yunu wi, "Dressed in Stone," who lived in that part of the country, and was always going about the mountains looking for some hunter to kill and eat. It was very hard to escape from him, because his stick guided him like a dog, and it was nearly as hard to kill him, because his whole body was covered with a skin of solid rock. If he came he would kill and eat them all, and there was only one way to save themselves. He could not bear to look upon a menstrual woman, and if they could find seven menstrual women to stand in the path as he came along the sight would kill him.

So they asked among all the women, and found seven who were sick in that way, and with one of them it had just begun. By the order of the medicine-man they stripped themselves and stood along the path where the old man would come. Soon they heard Nun yunu wi coming through the woods, feeling his way with his stone cane. He came along the trail to where the first woman was standing, and as soon as he saw her he started and cried out: "Yu! my grandchild; you are in a very bad state!" He hurried past her, but in a moment he met the next woman, and cried out again: "Yu! my child; you are in a terrible way," and hurried past her, but now he was vomiting blood. He hurried on and met the third and the fourth and the fifth woman, but with each one that he saw his step grew weaker until when he came to the last one, with whom the sickness had just begun, the blood poured from his mouth and he fell down on the trail.

Then the medicine-man drove seven sourwood stakes through his body and pinned him to the ground, and when night came they piled great logs over him and set fire to them, and all the people gathered around to see. Nun yunu wi was a great ada wehi and knew many secrets, and now as the fire came close to him, he began to talk, and told them the medicine for all kinds of sickness. At midnight he began to sing, and sang the hunting songs for calling up the bear and the deer and all the animals of the woods and the mountains. As the blaze grew hotter his voice sank low and lower, until at last when daylight came, the logs were a heap of white ashes and the voice was still.

Then the medicine-man told them to rake off the ashes, and where the body had lain they found only a large lump of red wa di paint and a magic u lunsu ti stone. He kept the stone for himself, and calling the people around him he painted them, on face and breast with the red wa di, and whatever each person prayed for while the painting was being done—whether for hunting success, for working skill, or for a long life—that gift was his.

TSUL KALU, THE SLANT-EYED GIANT

A long time ago a widow lived with her one daughter at the old town of Kanuga on Pigeon river. The girl was of age to marry, and her mother used to talk with her a good deal, and tell her she must be sure to take no one but a good hunter for a husband, so that they would have some one to take care of them and would always have plenty of meat in the house. The girl said such a man was hard to find, but her mother advised her not to be in a hurry, and to wait until the right one came.

Now the mother slept in the house while the girl slept outside in the asi. One dark night a stranger came to the asi wanting to court the girl, but she told him her mother would let her marry no one but a good hunter. "Well," said the stranger, "I am a great hunter," so she let him come in, and he stayed all night. Just before day he said he must go back now to his own place, but that he had brought some meat for her mother, and she would find it outside. Then he went away and the girl had not seen him. When day came she went out and found there a deer, which she brought into the house to her mother, and told her it was a present from her new sweetheart. Her mother was pleased, and they had deersteaks for breakfast.

He came again the next night, but again went away before daylight, and this time he left two deer outside. The mother was more pleased this time, but said to her daughter, "I wish your sweetheart would bring us some wood." Now wherever he might be, the stranger knew their thoughts, so when he came the next time he said to the girl, "Tell your mother I have brought wood"; and when she looked out in the morning there were several great trees lying in front of the door, roots and branches and all. The old woman was angry, and said, "He might have brought us some wood that we could use instead of whole trees that we can't split, to litter up the road with brush." The hunter knew what she said, and the next time he came he brought nothing, and when they looked out in the morning the trees were gone and there was no wood at all, so the old woman had to go after some herself.

Almost every night he came to see the girl, and each time he brought a deer or some other game, but still he always left before daylight. At last her mother said to her, "Your husband always leaves before daylight. Why don't he wait? I want to see what kind of a son-in-law I have." When the girl told this to her husband he said he could not let the old woman see him, because the sight would frighten her. "She wants to see you, anyhow," said the girl, and began to cry, until at last he had to consent, but warned her that her mother must not say that he looked frightful (usga se ti yu).

The next morning he did not leave so early, but stayed in the asi, and when it was daylight the girl went out and told her mother. The old woman came and looked in, and there she saw a great giant, with long slanting eyes (tsul kalu), lying doubled up on the floor, with his head against the rafters in the left-hand corner at the back, and his toes scraping the roof in the right-hand corner by the door. She gave only one look and ran back to the house, crying, Usga se ti yu! Usga se ti yu!

Tsul kalu was terribly angry. He untwisted himself and came out of the asi, and said good-bye to the girl, telling her that he would never let her mother see him again, but would go back to his own country. Then he went off in the direction of Tsunegun yi.

Soon after he left the girl had her monthly period. There was a very great flow of blood, and the mother threw it all into the river. One night after the girl had gone to bed in the asi her husband came again to the door and said to her, "It seems you are alone," and asked where was the child. She said there had been none. Then he asked where was the blood, and she said her mother had thrown it into the river. She told just where the place was, and he went there and found a small worm in the water. He took it up and carried it back to the asi, and as he walked it took form and began to grow, until, when he reached the asi, it was a baby girl that he was carrying. He gave it to his wife and said, "Your mother does not like me and abuses our child, so come and let us go to my home." The girl wanted to be with her husband, so, after telling her mother good-bye, she took up the child and they went off together to Tsunegun yi.

Now, the girl had an older brother, who lived with his own wife in another settlement, and when he heard that his sister was married he came to pay a visit to her and her new husband, but when he arrived at Kanuga his mother told him his sister had taken her child and gone away with her husband, nobody knew where. He was sorry to see his mother so lonely, so he said he would go after his sister and try to find her and bring her back. It was easy to follow the footprints of the giant, and the young man went along the trail until he came to a place where they had rested, and there were tracks on the ground where a child had been lying and other marks as if a baby had been born there. He went on along the trail and came to another place where they had rested, and there were tracks of a baby crawling about and another lying on the ground. He went on and came to where they had rested again, and there were tracks of a child walking and another crawling about. He went on until he came where they had rested again, and there were tracks of one child running and another walking. Still he followed the trail along the stream into the mountains, and came to the place where they had rested again, and this time there were footprints of two children running all about, and the footprints can still be seen in the rock at that place.

Twice again he found where they had rested, and then the trail led up the slope of Tsunegun yi, and he heard the sound of a drum and voices, as if people were dancing inside the mountain. Soon he came to a cave like a doorway in the side of the mountain, but the rock was so steep and smooth that he could not climb up to it, but could only just look over the edge and see the heads and shoulders of a great many people dancing inside. He saw his sister dancing among them and called to her to come out. She turned when she heard his voice, and as soon as the drumming stopped for a while she came out to him, finding no trouble to climb down the rock, and leading her two little children by the hand. She was very glad to meet her brother and talked with him a long time, but did not ask him to come inside, and at last he went away without having seen her husband.

Several other times her brother came to the mountain, but always his sister met him outside, and he could never see her husband. After four years had passed she came one day to her mother's house and said her husband had been hunting in the woods near by, and they were getting ready to start home tomorrow, and if her mother and brother would come early in the morning they could see her husband. If they came too late for that, she said, they would find plenty of meat to take home. She went back into the woods, and the mother ran to tell her son. They came to the place early the next morning, but Tsul kalu and his family were already gone. On the drying poles they found the bodies of freshly killed deer hanging, as the girl had promised, and there were so many that they went back and told all their friends to come for them, and there were enough for the whole settlement.

Still the brother wanted to see his sister and her husband, so he went again to the mountain, and she came out to meet him. He asked to see her husband, and this time she told him to come inside with her. They went in as through a doorway, and inside he found it like a great townhouse. They seemed to be alone, but his sister called aloud, "He wants to see you," and from the air came a voice, "You can not see me until you put on a new dress, and then you can see me." "I am willing," said the young man, speaking to the unseen spirit, and from the air came the voice again, "Go back, then, and tell your people that to see me they must go into the townhouse and fast seven days, and in all that time they must not come out from the townhouse or raise the war whoop, and on the seventh day I shall come with new dresses for you to put on so that you can all see me."

The young man went back to Kanuga and told the people. They all wanted to see Tsul kalu, who owned all the game in the mountains, so they went into the townhouse and began the fast. They fasted the first day and the second and every day until the seventh—all but one man from another settlement, who slipped out every night when it was dark to get something to eat and slipped in again when no one was watching. On the morning of the seventh day the sun was just coming up in the east when they heard a great noise like the thunder of rocks rolling down the side of Tsunegun yi. They were frightened and drew near together in the townhouse, and no one whispered. Nearer and louder came the sound until it grew into an awful roar, and everyone trembled and held his breath—all but one man, the stranger from the other settlement, who lost his senses from fear and ran out of the townhouse and shouted the war cry.

At once the roar stopped and for some time there was silence. Then they heard it again, but as if it were going farther away, and then farther and farther, until at last it died away in the direction of Tsunegun yi, and then all was still again. The people came out from the townhouse, but there was silence, and they could see nothing but what had been seven days before.

Still the brother was not disheartened, but came again to see his sister, and she brought him into the mountain. He asked why Tsul kalu had not brought the new dresses, as he had promised, and the voice from the air said, "I came with them, but you did not obey my word, but broke the fast and raised the war cry." The young man answered, "It was not done by our people, but by a stranger. If you will come again, we will surely do as you say." But the voice answered, "Now you can never see me." Then the young man could not say any more, and he went back to Kanuga.

The character in the preceding story, called Tsul kalu by Mooney, is more commonly called by Cherokees a name that comes close in pronunciation to the spelling of the Anglicized version, "Jutac-ulla." The emphasis is on the final syllable.

The implications of the preceding story to the discussion of the more sinister side of Cherokee medicine are admittedly subtle, although the attachment of Tsul kalu, or Jutaculla, to the spirit world is obvious enough. I have included the tale here because of the insistence of many Cherokees that much of the medicine used today was given to the Cherokees by Jutaculla. There seems to be no story extant that tells how this happened. There is, however, the mysterious "Jutaculla Rock" near Cullowhee, North Carolina. (Cullowhee is shortened and Anglicized from Jutaculla-whee, or Jutaculla's Place.) The rock is "a large soapstone slab covered with rude carvings, which, according to the same tradition, are scratches made by the giant in jumping from his farm on the mountain to the creek below" (Mooney, *Myths of the Cherokee*).

The rock is partially underground, and clearly some of the markings continue on beneath the surface. The face of the rock, much too big to jump across, is literally covered with a variety of markings, some resembling handprints, some slightly curved crosses, some circular indentations as if water dripped there for a long time, some almost forming faces. As Mooney says, the markings, in the Cherokee memory, were clearly put there by Jutaculla. Some say that if we could but read them, they would tell us much, much more than we now know.

Taken together, the stories above give us several possible origins of the kind of medicine under consideration here. Is one story right and the others wrong? Are all of them right? Or are they all metaphors for some things that might have happened along the way, things about which we will never know? Take them how you will.

2

Interview with Little Bear

I first began this book on May 29, 1997, at the John Little Bear home on Stick Ross Mountain just outside of Tahlequah, Oklahoma, the historic capital city of the Cherokee Nation. Tahlequah was established by the Cherokee Nation as its capital in 1839, just after the infamous Trail of Tears. On the occasion of this first meeting, I had little idea what I was embarking on with Little Bear. We sat together in lawn chairs in the middle of his front yard. I turned on a tape recorder, and the following conversation resulted.

Conley: *Well, I guess the first question is how long has your home been right up here, your family home?*

Little Bear: Well, my home been around here in Cherokee County for years, around Qualls, Cookson. Been all around in there, our home has. My grandmother, great-grandfather before my grandmother, he was a doctor. And then my grandmother, she's doctored people for I don't know how many years. She's 115 years old now, and she's still doing things for the people. And the medicine was handed down to me so many years back. I do the medicine work also, for the people, you know, helping people along with the things I'm supposed to do for them, what I was told to do. And I'm carrying it on so my sons can open up for what they can handle it. But it's usually one boy out of a family or a girl, medicine's handed down to them. We watch that kid as it's growing up, and we hand the medicine down to that kid. That's the way it's been done for years. You know, we been watched over to see if it's the one that's going to be able to take care of it.

31

John Little Bear

How old were you when you knew that this was going to be your life?

Well, I guess I knowed from the time I was about five or six years old. They started in teaching me things back at that time about the medicine, how it was done and things thisaway, and as I growed up, they told me I didn't fool with it until I got to a certain age. When I got to that certain age, they told me it was time for me to come home and start helping the people, so I started helping the people slowly, and they slowly brought me into the medicine stronger, and when I reached the age of fifty years old, everything was handed to me, and they told me, okay, now it's up to you to go on with the people, and I been doing this for several years now with the people. I been really doing the medicine, stepping up, for about twenty some years, and now it's when I reached the age of fifty everything was handed to me, and they told me it was my time. That's what I do now—with the people.

I had another thought, but I lost it.

That's just like the sweat that we do. I couldn't put in a sweat till I was age of forty-five. That's when, oh, the way they did it. They reached that age of forty-five years old, and then they put in a sweat. And that's the same way I was brought up to do it, up to that time that I put in a sweat, and we used to sweat and clean ourselves up. We also used the medicine they call the redroot, cleaning ourselves up. And there's still things that we use through the sweat to clean ourselves up with, and I would say, after you used the sweat and everything else, the way a person feels, they feel such a strain, but the next day you feel like a new man or a new woman.

Yeah. I know your grandmother's a medicine person. You say your grandfather was?

My great-grandfather.

Your great-grandfather.

Yeah.

Your grandmother's father?

My grandmother's father. Yeah. And his father before him. There was just one woman. Ever. And that was my grandmother's the one. She's the one's 115 years old now, and she's held the medicine all these years what she still holds it, but I been turned loose with it, but like every time I go up there and talk with her and things like that, it's something new that I didn't know anything about, and I thought I knowed everything about it, but it's always something new about it, and she'll teach me. Here I am over fifty years old, way over, and I'm still learning things from her.

Well, that's the way it should be. I guess nobody ever knows everything.

No. That's right. We ever get to know everything, I guess that's when we—gone.

Where did your people come from? Did they come over the Trail of Tears?

Yeah. They came over the Trail of Tears. My great-great-grandfather was and my grandmother's father, and they all came over on the Trail of Tears, and there was two twins that started out as medicine people. They came through on the Trail of Tears, and they're the ones carried the medicine from the Carolinas back here, and their medicine's always been here in Cherokee County. My great-great-grandfather doctored people. He lived up around Qualls, up around the Cookson Mountains, up in there, and after he passed away, my grandfather had took it over, and he carried on with it, then my grandmother, now it's me. And there's a younger boy, my son, that we're all watching, my grandmother and myself's watching right now, to hand the medicine down to him.

It ain't been but just one woman that's held the medicine, and she was watched over all these years, all them years, but it's gone back to the man again.

Well, tell me about the medicine in general. I know there's people that do bad things to people and people who don't do that. How would you explain that whole business of the medicine to somebody who just doesn't even know what we're talking about?

Okay. Bad medicine what is done toward a person can be different, in several different ways. It can be fixed into tobacco, it can be fixed into different things that you can put into a person's home, or scattered in their yard, and what it does to our body and our minds is affected by this, and when this is done toward a person, that person get to where he's sickly, he'll get to a point where—he might have a good job—he'll lose his job, he'll lose his family. He'll lose everything that he's got. And it'll be just because this other person over here got jealous, 'cause this person here's got what he's got, and the bad medicine's been used to make that person lose everything.

Okay, when they do things like that, when they have all these things happen, they usually come to another person, another doctor, another doctor'll check everything out. What I'm saying about checking things out, a lot of the times this man will go to the water to check it, or we'll go in our room, our medicine room, and check to see if the crystal—we use a crystal to check things—and it will tell us about what's going on with that person's life. Okay, you ask this crystal about things, what you want to find out, and it'll tell you about things. Okay, then you come back and tell this person what's going on. This person might not have told you that much about what's happening to him, but everything you ask that crystal, it'll tell you about that person's life. Okay, you come to that person and tell him what's going on and everything. He'll start telling you, yeah, that's what's happening. That's what's going on. And then you tell that person what he's going to have to have, tobacco, or whether he's going to have to go to the sweat to get this thing off of him, and then you take the tobacco and fix it. I will take and use the sweat and tobacco to get that person back the way he's supposed to be, to where his life will go back together, bring his family back, get his, maybe not the same job but a better job, to where that person can start coming up in the world again.

Indian medicine is strange, it's, uh, some people think it's, oh, witchcraft or things like that. Indian medicine's not witchcraft. It's a complete different thing. The witchcraft is, uh, how would you say? It's done like black magic. And Indian medicine is not done with, you know, black magic. It's done with the things that we was taught through the years, different things that we was taught. I can't tell you how to do it, or anything, 'cause there was some that was taught to us, they told us not to ever tell anybody what it was. And how to do it. 'Cause we'd have everybody running around here as medicine men.

That's right.

There's a lot of them that wouldn't take care of it, that's like some of the younger generation. Old people has passed away, and the younger generation thought, well, you know, they done it, but they didn't watch the word, they wouldn't hand it to them 'cause they wouldn't take care of the things they was supposed to take care of. They had picked up the books, translating them back, and they doing this medicine and things like that, and this younger generation, they, uh, checking things out, and they hurting people with it. And it's not supposed to be done that way. We get a lot of them out there think, well, you know, hey, I done this, I done that, now I'm a medicine man, but they don't know how to take care of themselves.

It's medicine like that can be turned around and hurt you, and there's a lot of these older ones that's still living. When something like that's done, they ain't going to think, well, that person's just practicing to try to see what it'll do. They going to turn around on that person. They going to put— He might be just a nineteen- or twenty-year-old man or twenty-five-year-old man, but he's fooling with this Indian medicine he shouldn't fool with. That Indian medicine man's going to see it, and he's going to hurt that person. And that's the things we watch out for. We look at things this way.

Where does the power come from?

The power is the prayer that we was taught. And it's, uh, different things that we was told to say into the medicine before we went on ahead and said the other songs into it. There's things that we call on: the Great Spirit. And also there's things what lives in the woods. We call on them. And these things are all brought together in one band of songs is sung into the medicine. That's the way they do it.

And the power still lays. It's like it was way back when our great-grandfathers and things like that had it. The power's still there. It's strong as it ever was. And the one that takes care of the medicine like it's supposed to be, the power always will be there.

I had a great-grandfather—I never met him. He died when he was thirty-two years old. He lived out at Crittenden and out at Lost City, out there. And they said two things about him. His father died before he was born. And they said because his father died before he was born, he was able to cure babies of the thrush.

Yeah.

He'd breathe in their mouths. Does that make sense to you?

Yeah. My family, my grandmother, had told me about things this-away. There was certain people was born before they seen their father, things thisaway, and they could do things thisaway, you know, breathe into a kid's mouth, things thisaway, and cure the blood. And, uh, there's a lot of truth to that, what you're talking about.

There's kids right today, they don't know they can do these things. They'd been born like that, their father's gone, passed away, you know, passed away and everything. There's kids like that right today, some of them's thataway. They don't know it.

The schools take that away from kids.

Yeah, a lot of it's been taken away from these kids from these schools. Just like myself when I first started to school, I couldn't talk English. First year of school, I couldn't hardly talk English. And, uh, where as I went to school through the years and everything, I picked up the English. And then, they didn't want us to talk our own language. They told us not to be talking. A lot of it was taken away, but we went home and things like that, and that's all they was talking to us, our own Indian language, and so, I kept up with mine. All these years, I've kept up with it.

And the old Cherokee language from the Carolinas is a lot different what we got here now. That's just like the English. You know, it's a slang English what we—what you all talk back here. The regular English back in England plus a like that, you know, it's a different English. That's the thing, we wrote the Cherokee language back there. It's a slang, slang language. But when we go to do our medicine, work with our medicine, things like that, we have to work with the old Cherokee language. 'Cause that's the way it was written, you know, in our books what our grandfathers, great-grandfathers has left us. We have to talk in our old language, we have—the Cherokee language.

When somebody like that James Mooney, that old ethnographer, went to Cherokee, North Carolina, back in the 1890s, he got a lot of information from those people. One old medicine man named Swimmer. And he wrote down all that stuff. Wrote it in Cherokee, and he translated it, and he published it in a government publication. Does that destroy that medicine?

Well, in translating it thataway, yeah, it does destroy it. It weakens it. It don't destroy it. It weakens it. But you can take another Indian, and he can pick that book up, where that was written in English, and he can put it back into Indian, put that medicine back up, 'cause it's no good unless it's written in the native language.

Well, a lot of that stuff has been recorded, you know. Mooney recorded way back when, and then, uh, Jack Kilpatrick and his wife went through this part of the country in the fifties and got a lot of that stuff from people and had it published in Cherokee and in the English translation.

Well, a lot of it was—some of it was weakened, but not that bad.

Okay.

It's like a guy that was down to Henrietta. He done the same thing what you saying they done. They wrote a book about, you know, the Indian medicine, what he knowed and things like that, but when they turn it around in the English language—English language to us is backwards—and if you try to do the Indian medicine in English, the whole thing'll turn around on you. It can't be done either to help a person out here or harm that person. But if it was turned around and put back in the old Indian language, it would work.

What about the old, old stories, you know, about characters like Flint, whatever, those old animal stories, monsters and what not. Are they explanations of beliefs or maybe—is it something philosophical or whatever in a concrete form for people to understand?

Well, if I could put it in English the way it'd be explained in the Indian way, you could understand it better, but I can't explain it real good. Indian people, or I would say about 75 percent of the Indian medicine men, can change theirselves into a different form. They can go out and check things. They can come to your house in a different form, and you wouldn't think anything about it. It might be a strange dog, you know, come around there and sneak around and . . . Every day he's gone. At nighttime's the only time you see him around there.

Well, that person is around there checking things. Sometimes they come there to do you harm. Or they'll come there to check out to see things what they done toward you if it's working. A lot of times they'll come as a owl. Sometimes they'll come as a crow. I say a crow, it's a raven. They come in different forms. It just depends on what that doctor wants to do like to come to your house with. That's some of the things that they do. Yeah, they can come to your house and you can be sound asleep and get a hold of you. You can't see them. You trying to do your level best to get away. You might be screaming and hollering, but nobody hears you. But these things like that, they can do it. They can do these things. I don't know how to do these things.

So it's possible that some of those old stories are just literal—true?

Yeah. There's a lot of truth to them. They can get you in the night like that. They can rob you of your life. That's what they call robbing you of your life. They can take so much of your life away from you. Where you may live to be maybe seventy-five or eighty years old, you might not live to be sixty. They take a lot of it away from you. That person been bothering right there several times, four or five times. That person starts to get sick, hard, weak, don't feel like doing anything. It's like, you know, I just feel like I want to give up. And that's what happens to a lot of them. They'll give up. Then somebody'll come along and say, hey, there's somebody following you, something's going on in your life. They'll take that person and bring him to a person like myself, or somebody like my grandmother, someone like that, and they'll doctor them up. Then he'll realize, hey, there was something going on. But that person usually if somebody's following them like that, they's usually scratches on them. And how they got those scratches nobody knows. They ain't been around brush. They ain't been around somebody to scratch them, anything like that. But they still end up with scratches on them. Look like claw marks.

(A second questioner) What's been done to me?

Well, I can't tell, right now in front of everybody. But it's things that's been done in your place of business. People hand you things, and you go ahead and accept it. It's things you got to watch out for. They can hand you something that's been fixed. And right away you stick it in your place of business, your business scatters. People get where they don't want to be around you. That's some of the things you got to watch out for. You don't want to just take something and put it in your place of business. You accept it, but take it outside and leave it outside. You going to see what this thing is they giving you, you know.

So if somebody gave me something, and especially if it was a surprise, I don't know why this guy gave me this thing, I could bring it to you and. . . .

Yeah, we could check it out.

Check it out? — Handling contaminators.

Lot of times they'll hand you tobacco and say, you can go ahead and use this. This is good. It'll make you feel good. But why would anybody just come out here and hand you tobacco? What I'm saying, you know, there's people out here that'll pretend to be your friend. They'll give you something, and you'll take it to your house. After a while your wife starts getting mad at you. Kids getting mad at you. People that you're accustomed to being around, they don't want to be around you. Okay, everything starts going down. What's happening here? You know, why is this happening to me? Then you think, ah, it's just a ordinary thing, 'cause you know, bad luck, bad luck. Okay, but why am I having all this bad luck? How come it's getting that bad? Something like that's been done. It ain't going to happen tomorrow. It ain't going to happen next week. It may be several weekends before anything like that happens. Okay, but when it happens, that rascal starts to be getting bad. You don't know which way to turn, don't know which way to go. You know, you just feel like giving up on everything. But just like he was saying. Why would anyone want to do those things? Jealousy.

You got all these people coming to you, asking, hey, do this, do this, how can we do this? Okay, you standing there talking, you say this is what we're going to do. That old boy who heard you, he wishes he was the same way, he wished they was coming to him. He just gets madder out of jealousy. Do something towards you. And the Indian people is the worst ones to do it towards each other.

Sort of like this guy one time. He bought him a new car. He had a good job. He was working his damn tail off, too. His wife working. Bought him a new car. Gave it to his wife. Then he bought a new pickup. He had a new pickup and a new car. Old boy ten miles down the road there, he used to be a real good friend of his, come to his house. I need to borrow $100. He loans the old boy $100. About a month later, the old boy brings the $100 back with the $100 fixed. He lost his job, he lost his wife, he lost his cars. He ended up walking.

The man now is just now getting back on his feet. I helped him, helped him, helped him. He's just now getting back up on his feet. His brother, they done him the same way. His brother almost died. He almost died. I started helping him. Got him back up. Everything. Now they picking on him again, trying to push him back down. But we're bringing that boy back up again. He was going to his office. He would pass out on the highway going down the highway. His own brother, his other brother, just said the hell with him. I don't want to have nothing to do with him. But this one brother, he stuck with him, stuck with him, stuck with him, stuck with him. The other boy ended up where he didn't have anything there for a while. Absolutely nothing. These boys used to have Lincolns, nice home, two, three cars setting in the yard. They had everything that they wanted.

I wish they were around here today so you could talk to them. They could tell you what things has happened to them. Well, they'll be around. They'll talk to you.

I had my doubts. People are hesitant to talk about medicine and about the details of troubles in their lives. Indian people especially are reticent about such things, in addition to just being tight-lipped around strangers. I had my doubts, but Little Bear was right. They did talk to me. In fact, no one I approached ever refused to talk to me.

3

A Very Brief Life Story

John Little Bear was born with a veil over his entire body. He won't say exactly when. He won't give his exact age. All he'll say is that it's within a few years of my own. When he was born, his mother was only seventeen years old, and she did not want the responsibility of a child. Little Bear was left with his grandparents. His grandmother was a well-known, respected, and sometimes feared medicine woman. He called his grandmother "Mama." When he started school, he could speak only Cherokee. He was into his second year before he began speaking any English. I've heard one of his relatives say that when Little Bear was a small child, he followed his grandmother around all over the place, even going into the woods with her when she was gathering herbs. All this time, of course, he was learning about the herbs and other things.

As a child, Little Bear could see into the future. He might see one of his playmates fall off of something, then blink his eyes and everything was all right, but the boy would fall later. At last he asked his grandfather about it. Grandfather told him it was because of the veil he had been born with.

He was about twelve years old when he finally asked his grandfather a question that had been troubling him for some time. He had two "aunts" who came around from time to time, and he felt a special affinity for one of them. He asked his grandfather why. His grandparents looked at one another, sat him down, and told him that the one he had the strongest feeling for was really his mother. One time his mother and grandmother were fighting, and Little Bear yelled out, "Mama, stop." Each woman thought that he was calling out to her. About two years later, his grandfather died.

Little Bear had a constant companion when he was growing up, his cousin Red. If Grandma wanted Little Bear to do something and he was feeling stubborn, she would tell Red to help her get Little Bear to do it. Sometimes it worked. But if Little Bear was still stubborn with Red and refused to do the thing that Grandma wanted done, Grandma would get mad at Red, too. "You two are just alike," she would say.

Little Bear and Red conceived a plan to make money. They started building rabbit cages to trap rabbits, and they built five of them, but then they got sidetracked "chasing women."

Little Bear had to haul water, and he would sling the bucket over on his back, but he had to cross a field in which a mean bull lived. If the bull caught sight of him, it would chase him, and the water would spill all over Little Bear's back. He decided that he'd had enough of that, and one day he said so. He went after water, and on the way back to the house he saw the bull. He ducked behind a tree, and when the bull came running, he stepped out and hit it with his fist right between the eyes. The bull dropped. Little Bear dropped down on it and started twisting its neck. The bull's owner came running to the rescue, shouting, "Don't kill my bull."

Grandma also kept a bunch of hogs, and one of them was a pet that would walk in and out of the house at will, looking for something to eat.

When Red was grown, he bought a trailer home, and Grandma let him put it on her property. Somewhere along the line, he says, he "got messed up," and he wound up over $700 behind on his payments. He was getting calls about it, and one day Grandma asked him what was bothering him. He didn't want to tell her, but she kept asking. Finally, he confessed. She always knew, he said. "Don't worry about it," she told him. "They're not going to take your trailer. They not even going to bother you about it."

Soon after that, they called again. Red answered the phone, but when he found out who was calling, he gave the phone to Grandma. "I want you to leave my grandson alone," she said. "Don't bother him no more."

And somehow, Red said, Grandma came up with the money for him.

Once, when he had been away for a time, Red came by Grandma's house. "Why haven't you been around?" she asked him.

"My head's been hurting me," he said.

"Come here," she said.

She had him come close to her and bend over. She spit on her hands and rubbed them together very fast. Then she clapped her hands against the sides of his head and held them there for perhaps five minutes. The headache was gone.

Often Grandma had Red go into the woods and gather herbs for her. He said she always offered to pay him, but he felt bad taking her money, so he would refuse. Then she'd get mad at him.

Red developed a drinking problem, and after he and Little Bear were grown and Little Bear had a grown son, Red and the son drank together. Once they got two pints of whiskey and were drinking out behind Grandma's house. They finished the first pint and were about to open the second when they heard Little Bear coming. Red tossed the pint to Little Bear's son, who quickly scraped out a hole by the house and tucked the pint away. They forgot about it.

Then one day Red was staggering down the road drunk, thinking that he was going to town. Little Bear's wife, Sally, pulled up behind him. She yelled at him to get into the car, and she drove him right back up to Grandma's house. "Here's your boy," she called out. "Drunk." Red went on into Grandma's house, as he said, "reeking." She told him to quit drinking. Then she got together with Little Bear, and they made a plan. Grandma told Red, "You're going to quit." She and Little Bear together made some medicine and put it in a pint of whiskey. She offered the pint to Red, and he took one swallow. It almost went down. Then he puked. He was sick for two or three days, and then, sure enough, he quit. Just to be certain, to test him, they were going somewhere not long after that, and they stopped at a store. Grandma gave

Red $3 and told him to go inside and get a six-pack of beer. It was a hot day.

"A cold beer would taste good right now," she said. Red took the $3 and started in to the store, but before he got there, he stopped. He went back to the car and gave her back the money. "Don't you think a cold beer would be good?" she asked him. "No," he said. "I don't need it. Water will be just fine."

Grandma had Red and Little Bear's son dig up a space for a garden close to the house, and the son ran into something he thought was a rock. He dug around some and finally came out with the pint of whiskey he had hidden from his father three years earlier. He retrieved it and opened it up, and a cloud of blue smoke came out of the bottle. They didn't drink that whiskey either.

Backing up a little, when Little Bear graduated from high school, he enlisted in the United States Marine Corps. His grandmother doctored him, and he was sent to Vietnam. On his return home, he was doctored again. Little Bear went to school at Okmulgee Tech and studied auto mechanics. He opened a shop in Tulsa and was doing well. Then one day his grandmother called him. "It's time to come home," she said. Little Bear knew what she meant. He had been trained for this his entire life. He gave up his business in Tulsa to return to Tahlequah and "work with the people."

Little Bear told me that the time comes in every medicine man's life when he has to pass a test. In his clan) the test is to get a horn from the great snake, the "King of All Snakes." When Little Bear returned to Tahlequah, Grandma told him that in order to be a medicine man, he would have to fight the Uk'ten' and get a piece of his horn. (See "The Uktena and the Ulunsu ti" and "The Red Man and the Uktena" in chapter 1.) Little Bear would have to go to the river and go down in the water where it lives to find it. Grandma told Little Bear when he came across the monster to look in its eyes and not look away until he had what he was after. "Grab hold of its antlers and don't let go until you have a piece of antler," she told him. She had a piece of the horn from her own fight years earlier. She showed it to Little Bear. She could close

Uk'ten', King of All Snakes

her fist around it, but she said that when she got it, it stuck out from her closed fist about three inches. It shrinks with time, and its power goes into the medicine person who possesses it. Little Bear said that he had seen her rub it and then rub her hands over her own face.

When the time came, Little Bear went to the river with his grandmother. They stood at the edge of the water, and she sang a song to call up the monster snake. Soon it appeared on the surface out in the middle of the river. Little Bear was afraid, but he did not hesitate. Grandma had prepared him. He waded into the water. As they drew close to one another, Little Bear looked the awesome creature in the eyes. He reached out with both hands and grabbed a piece of antler in each. The Uk'ten' thrashed around and screamed, but Little Bear hung on tight and kept looking the monster in the eyes. It took him down under the water, and Little Bear could see some bluffs under there. The snake tried to knock him off against the bluffs. They came back up. Then they went under again. They surfaced again, still struggling, and then they went down for a third time. At last the snake gave a violent twist, and the piece of antler Little Bear was holding on to with one hand snapped off. The Uk'ten' made a horrible noise. As Little Bear let go with his other hand, it turned and swam away. He and Grandma could see the wake it left in the water. Little Bear made it to the surface gasping for air. He was clutching his prize. He was ready.

In the pages that follow, individuals' names have been changed. I should also mention that although Little Bear's real Cherokee name is indeed Little Bear, he is not generally known by that name.

4

The Beginnings of This Book

One Saturday afternoon as people were gathered at Little Bear's house for a sweat or just waiting to see him for help, Little Bear went out on the porch and made an announcement. "This is Mr. Conley," he said. "He's writing a book about me, and I want you to talk to him." The stories that follow were told to me by the people who go to Little Bear with problems. He said they would talk to me, and they did. Some would hardly stop once they got started, and others were much more reticent. But they all had stories to tell. These tales were gleaned over a period of six years.

Much has happened during that time. Little Bear's grandmother died, and Little Bear called me and asked me to write something about her and to read it at the funeral. I did so with a great sense of humility. Following the funeral, everyone who participated gathered in the yard at his grandmother's house. We had to be washed off. One of Little Bear's sons stood with a bucket of medicine and a gourd dipper, and we lined up to take our turns. We washed off with the medicine, over our heads, our arms, and our feet. Then we ate.

Little Bear's cousin Red had grown up with Grandma and with Little Bear. With Grandma's death, Red's life fell apart. Grandma had always been there for him. Even if he was not around her house, she always knew if something was wrong with him. It took him some time to realize that he had to do things for himself, to take care of himself. At last, then, things began to come together again for him, but he told me, "She'll still help me, if I pray to her." He is not the only one in the family who still depends on her. One of Little Bear's sons has told me that she comes to him when he needs help, and Little Bear himself still communes with her.

Since the funeral, Little Bear has gone into Grandma's house. He found her medicine books in a bucket under the bed, and the bucket was hot to the touch. Little Bear took it to the woods and hid it. And she has visited him on more than one occasion. He's still learning from her. Life goes on. There are people who need help. Here are some of their stories.

5

Sally's Story

It seems appropriate to begin with Sally's story. Sally is Little Bear's wife, and she is very much a part of his life and work as a medicine man. Sally is, in fact, a medicine person herself, and though she seems content to appear to function as Little Bear's helper, she does make medicine and doctor people herself. Her father and two of her mother's brothers were Creek medicine men, and as she was growing up, she learned from them.

Sally told me that when she was a little girl, her father told her she was going to meet a medicine man when she was twelve years old. She met several medicine men before meeting Little Bear, although several members of her family already knew him. Her brother took her with him to Tahlequah one time, and that was when she actually met Little Bear. When she met him that first time, she told me, she felt something in his arms, "like a powerful thing that went up my arm when I shook hands with him." They talked for a while, and Little Bear went in the back room to "read on it." Sally said, "Everything was right on the button. It was scary to hear about what he told."

Later, when Sally moved in with Little Bear, she met his grandmother, and Sally was afraid of her. "I guess it was the powerful look she had." Then later, Grandma asked Sally to read on her. Sally was shocked. Grandma knew that Sally knew how to read on people and knew how to make medicine as well. After that, Sally and Little Bear started working together on medicine. At first it was difficult, because they were brought up strict, not to listen to others. Little Bear kept telling her, though, to sit and listen, and she did. From then on, together, they took care of people the way Sally's father had taught her, and they've been working together ever since.

I was sitting on the porch one day with Little Bear and Sally and a few other people. Little Bear said that it was about time he got back to work. He said to Sally, "Come on, Baby. I need your help."

"I got everything ready for you," she answered. "Just go do your stuff."

"No. Come on," he said. "I need you back there with me."

Sally sometimes works with the women. Sometimes she conducts a sweat lodge ceremony. Mostly, she tells me, "We just always work together." When she was done talking with me, she asked me if I wanted to talk with their youngest son, Alex. "He's getting that way," she said. "He reads. He knows a few little stuff."

6

Alex

Sally sent Alex in to see me. She had already told me that he's the seventh son. I asked the boy how old he was. He answered that he was twelve years old. I asked him if he was learning things from his father. He said that he was, and then he said, "I know how to read." He was not talking about reading books. I asked if he was learning anything else. "I help people when they're hurting," he said. I asked if he meant when they have a sore shoulder or a sore arm or something like that, and he agreed.

"Can you tell me what you do?" I asked.

"I just put that thing on my hand, and then I put my hand on them where they're hurting," he said. "I sing a song." He wouldn't say what "that thing" is. He did say that he's learning the songs and that he's learning how to disappear and how to fly. Alex is the next generation of medicine men, and I believe that he's going to be a good one.

Ordinarily, though, he is just out playing with the other kids, doing all the things that kids his age do, playing ball, wrestling, making jaunts into the woods and returning with captured small animals.

7

Frank's Story

Frank was going for help to a well-known, respected Cherokee medicine man, but nothing in his life was improving. He had a girlfriend, and they were planning to get married, but after two and a half years she left him. The medicine man Frank was going to told him that he could not help him. "You have a bullshit philosophy," the man said, "and I can't help you anymore. If you want something, just take it. How do you think I got everything I have?" Frank said that he couldn't do that. The man said, "I can't make you any more medicine because you won't use it." Frank said, "When I use the medicine, it gets ten times worse." The medicine was turning around and making things worse. And the people who were doing it to Frank knew that.

Frank had heard of Little Bear's grandmother, so he went to see her. Before he told her anything, she told Frank everything that had happened to him. She told him further about things that were going to happen. She fixed some medicine for him. Frank's girlfriend came back but only stayed a few days.

Frank went back up on the hill, but he told a member of Grandmother's family that he was having trouble talking to her. "Is there someone I can talk to?" he asked. She told him to talk to John Little Bear, the old woman's grandson. John Little Bear's house was just down the road from his grandmother's house, and Frank found Little Bear outside mowing the lawn. Little Bear stopped his work and sat down to visit with Frank. Frank told him his whole long story. His girlfriend had left him—twice. A local banker was embezzling money from Frank and had left him in financial ruin, and Frank had wasted away from 210 pounds to 160 pounds in thirty days. Little Bear listened to the story, and then he ""checked it out." He read on Frank.

Later, Little Bear told Frank that someone was trying to kill him. He said, "You need to clean yourself up." He told him to go home and come back the following Monday. When Frank returned, Little Bear had prepared medicine. He had Frank drink the medicine out in the middle of the road. The medicine made Frank woozy, and then it caused him to vomit. When it was all over, Frank felt suddenly much better. He could see more clearly. Little Bear prepared more medicine and told Frank what to do with it. He also told Frank that this process was going to take some time. Weeks passed.

Frank was able to return to work. He moved from Tulsa to Tahlequah. Months passed. At last, it became clear what had been going on. A cult member had wanted Frank's girlfriend, and he had gone to a medicine man for help. By the time Frank had gotten involved with Little Bear, there were four cult members and three medicine people on the other side "fighting" Frank. Before long, there were over twenty medicine people against him. Some of them were the very ones Frank had gone to earlier for help.

Little Bear began talking with Frank about the sweats. He asked Frank if he wanted to build a fire for him. Frank said, "Yes. If that's what you want me to do." That was the beginning of Frank's work with the sweats. Some of the medicine people who had been working against Frank died. The cult members backed off. Things had gotten much better for Frank. He said they were going well, but only so far. Then they stopped.

Little Bear continued "checking things out." He worked for a month. Then one day he told Frank, "I finally found it." The problem had been that Little Bear had been looking at living people. The bad medicine that had been tormenting Frank had been put on his family, put in their blood, years earlier by medicine people who were no longer living. They had taken it with them when they died. Little Bear told Frank to go ask his father if "he ever got into a fight with an old man over some cows."

Frank got the story from his father. When Frank was a small child, his father and his uncle had owned some cows. Six of the cows strayed onto a neighbor's property. During an argument that resulted, Frank's uncle pulled a shotgun on their neighbor, an old man. No shots were fired, but the old man was furious. He went to a well-known medicine man for revenge. The medicine man "put it in the family blood to be passed along." The medicine on Frank was old, Little Bear said. "Old, old, old." It had taken that old-time medicine person a full year to put it in place.

Then Frank recalled a dream from his childhood. Two trees had grown together in the corner of a fence. Frank was up in the tree. All around him for as far as he could see, the ground was covered with blacksnakes. When he remembered the dream, he told it to Little Bear. "That was when it happened," Little Bear told him. "You were the first one in your family to see it." What had followed for Frank and for other members of his family had been no success and general misery. Little Bear said it was a miracle that Frank was still alive. "A normal person would have blowed his brains out."

Little Bear checked further. In the meantime, other medicine people were being brought in on the other side. Frank was also making new enemies, people who were jealous of his new position with Little Bear in helping with the sweats. In addition to the sweats, Frank was taking four different kinds of medicine four times a day. He lived the life of a hermit, staying away from family and friends in order to protect them from the medicine that was attacking him. He told Little Bear, "They're teaching me. They're making me strong."

"I will fight with you," Little Bear told him, "if we have to fight to the death. They won't walk over you no more."

A year passed by with Little Bear working and helping and things getting better a little at a time. At last, he saw the way to get rid of it. Use the sweats. Burn it out of the blood. Four years later, Little Bear and Frank are still working on it. It will take time to get it clear out of the family.

Today, Frank is strong, comfortable, and confident. He takes other people through the sweats for Little Bear. Taking care of different groups, Frank himself goes through the sweats as many as fifteen times a day. In so doing, he is not only cleaning others off but cleaning himself as well.

As a result of the years of suffering, fighting back, and studying with Little Bear, Frank has achieved a certain serenity and wisdom. He has also realized that he has always seen things. Little Bear told him once, "The medicine has always been with you." Frank says, "John got me to where I could actually live with myself and understand myself and be at peace with myself." He says, "I always stopped and looked at things, but now I know why I stop and look at things."

An intense sensitivity has also developed in Frank. He found that he could not go through the main entrance of the local Wal-Mart store, but he can enter through the garden center with no problems. When he asked Little Bear about that, Little Bear told him that there was an underground stream that ran beneath the main entrance. Frank cannot walk comfortably against that stream. And walking on turned ground causes his legs to cramp. "There are things I can't do and places I can't go," he says, "because of being doctored to help people."

And Frank stands out in a crowd. Sometimes, he says, people notice him and think he has a superior air about him and dislike him for that. But Little Bear had said, "You will have people that will come up and ask you things." A total stranger approached him in a café and asked, "Can you tell me who my real dad is?" Another once said, "I was supposed to go home, but I'm supposed to talk to you."

He is particularly susceptible to a woman in her monthly cycle. He sat down in a chair on Little Bear's front porch one day and immediately began fidgeting. He felt as if he had suddenly developed a terrible rash. He asked Little Bear what was wrong with him, and Little Bear laughed.

"You finally found you one," Little Bear said.

A woman in her cycle had been sitting in that chair. Little Bear told Frank to go clean himself up. (Recall the tale recorded by James Mooney about Nun yunu wi and what it was that killed him.)

8

George's Story

George's family had come for some years to Little Bear's grandmother for help, and when Little Bear began practicing, George also sought help from Little Bear. He had known Little Bear for fifteen or sixteen years at the time he told me this tale, and this is the way it all got started.

George had a little daughter five or six years old. The little girl had developed some kind of infection, and George had taken her to Hillcrest Medical Center in Tulsa. She had a high fever and couldn't walk. An X-ray taken at Hillcrest showed a black spot inside her. Exploratory surgery failed to reveal the cause of the spot. The doctor told George, "I can't figure out what it is. We're going to have to give her a few days of recovery and then go back in again and find out."

A friend took George to see Little Bear's grandmother. Grandmother fixed some medicine and told George what to do with it. "She'll be out of there in four days," Grandmother said. "Don't let them cut on her again." George agreed. He went back to his daughter in the hospital and used the medicine as he'd been told. After four days, he asked the little girl, "Are you ready to get up and start walking around?"

"I can't walk," she said.

"Well now," said George, "you want to go get some ice cream?"

"Yes."

"Well then, you're going to have to walk."

"Daddy, I can't walk."

"Yeah, you can. Don't worry about it. You can."

She had a little purse she carried, and George picked it up.

"Come with me," he said. He picked her up and stood her on the floor. She started walking. In the hallway, the doctor encountered the two walking along side by side. He stopped them and told George, "We need to keep her in here. We have to go back in."

"No," said George. "I don't want you to."

"We have to keep her so we can watch her."

"I can watch her at home," said George. He took her home, and she had a complete recovery. The little girl is now fully grown.

9

Martha Jane

Martha Jane told me that there's nothing wrong with her, but I believe that was just her way of not talking about herself. She just brings other people up to see Little Bear, she said. She had a young woman with her, and all she would say is that "she has female problems." Little Bear helped her out with roots and herbs. He also made medicine for luck and protection.

Martha Jane told me about the time she had been sitting in her home holding her brother's grandbaby. The baby kept fighting. Martha Jane asked her, "What's wrong?"

The baby looked up and answered, "That one. That booger was trying to take me outside." Martha Jane couldn't see anyone or anything, but she believed the baby. (There is a certain kind of "witch" in Cherokee belief, which, according to Mooney, "is supposed to go about chiefly under cover of darkness, and hence is called su na yi eda hi, 'the night goer.'" This witch is believed to steal years from the lives of others to add to its own life, and its favorite victims are old people and children.) Martha Jane took the baby to see Little Bear. He prepared some tobacco for Martha Jane and gave her some water in which certain herbs had been boiled to bathe the baby in. Little Bear told Martha Jane, "If that thing had taken the baby outside, you'd never see her again." But the medicine worked, and the child was not bothered anymore.

10

Sonny's Story

Sonny told me that he goes to see Little Bear to take care of his mind, body, and spirit and to keep his blood pressure down. He goes to the sweats to rejuvenate his body and for his general well-being. The human body is like a sponge, he told me. It soaks up everything. He goes into the sweat regularly. The sweat cleans it all up again. I have been in the sweat on more than one occasion with Sonny. But his association with Little Bear began for more specific reasons.

Over twenty years ago, he had gone to see Little Bear's grandmother because his wrist was hurting him. She told him it had been "witched," and she helped him with it. Then in 1995, he was having problems again. There was never enough money, and his legs were starting to bother him. He couldn't find a medicine man he could trust or who would help him. His back was out of joint. He kept having visions of John Little Bear, whom he had met those many years ago when he had seen Little Bear's grandmother. These visions were all off in a certain specific direction. Sonny didn't know Little Bear's name though, just the family name. He searched the Internet for addresses and phone numbers, went to the telephone book and looked up the family name, and called everyone on the list until Little Bear answered the phone. Sonny recognized the voice. Right away, he went to see him and found that Little Bear was living in the same direction as he had seen in his visions. Little Bear snapped his back back into place. Looking into Sonny's problems, Little Bear discovered that Sonny's in-laws were trying to ruin Sonny financially. He gave Sonny redroot to drink and tobacco to smoke, and Sonny began

going to the sweats as often as he could. (He lives in Oklahoma City.) In a couple of weeks, Sonny says, he could feel the difference.

Once, Little Bear took Sonny and his brother to the water for a treatment meant to wash away anything that was bad. Little Bear and his wife also went to Sonny's house in the city to doctor the house. That same day, again, Sonny says, he could tell the difference almost immediately. Now Sonny visits Little Bear and goes to the sweats regularly just to keep in balance, and his whole family relies on Little Bear and his wife to help them with their special gifts. Sonny looks at Little Bear as a brother and his wife as a sister. They are both good people, Sonny says. In addition, in going to Little Bear's house, he meets other interesting people. He goes for his health and well-being and for the health and well-being of his family, but it's also a social occasion.

11

Henry's Story

Henry told me that when he was younger, he used to get together with friends and get drunk a lot. During the course of his revels, he met a young woman, and being drunk, they let nature take its course. Over a period of time, two children resulted from these shenanigans. But Henry became very fond of his children, and the mother continued using drugs and drinking. She would not agree to joint custody. Then she went to court and won the case for child support from Henry, including back child support. One of Henry's cousins recommended that Henry go to see Little Bear.

Henry began paying child support, but the back child support was a difficulty. He was told that the most they would allow him was three years to get it all paid. He began using the medicine that Little Bear prepared for him, tobacco to be smoked in a pipe. When he went to court, he was given six years to get caught up on the payments. But he's not through. He's still going to see Little Bear, because he wants custody of the children. "You people," he told the social workers, "are worried about money, and I'm worried about my kids."

Henry is married now to someone else and has a little boy, but he wants his other children because their mother drinks and uses drugs. He told me that he feels very hopeful. "Things are going my way."

12

The Sweat

The purpose of the sweat is spiritual cleansing or purification. The fire that is used to heat the rocks was brought from North Carolina. Frank says, "It's as big a part of you as you are of it. It's a living spirit. Treat it with respect. It can be your best friend or your worst nightmare." He says further, "We try to stay close to the old ways." Outside the sweat lodge is a circle. The fire is in the center of the circle. The circle has a ridge or wall with an opening or a door. The wall should not be stepped over or even reached across. The door must be used to go inside the circle or to go back outside. No one goes inside the circle except the man who is tending the fire, heating the rocks, and bringing the rocks from the fire into the sweat lodge. He goes in and out through the opening in the wall, and whether he walks around the fire inside the wall or outside the wall, he walks around in a counterclockwise direction. Everyone else who walks around the circle also walks in a counterclockwise direction.

The lodge itself is but a few feet away from the circle. It's also built in a circle. Overall, it's a dome, covered with some heavy material, canvas usually. Little Bear is trying to get some buffalo robes for covering. It has a flap door. When the people go inside for a sweat, the door is closed. Depending on the weather and the time of day, it can be totally dark inside. Even if it is not totally dark, when the medicine is poured over the hot rocks, the rising steam can be so thick that it is impossible to see the person sitting next to you.

When Frank takes a person into the sweat, he feels everything that other person is feeling, physical and emotional. When he took a man recovering from triple bypass surgery into the sweat, he felt

The sweat lodge. Drawing by Murv Jacob.

like he was having a heart attack. He has surprised people many times when they come out of the sweat by perhaps putting his hand up to his head and asking someone, "Did that pain in your head go away?" Once, he asked someone, "When did you break your leg?" Those who have been through the sweats with Frank several times are used to that. They simply answer the question matter-of-factly. "Heat is not bad," Frank says. "It's what's on the person that's bad. If you feel something cool on your legs while you're in there, something's going on. Evil is cold."

When the sweat is done, Frank leaves the lodge first, taking with him anything bad that the sweat has removed from the people in there. When he throws open the door, he sends it all back where it came from.

One time, after some particularly hard fights, Frank couldn't take any more. He had people waiting to go through the sweats, but he went in to see Little Bear and told him that he just couldn't handle it. He had to go home. Little Bear took the last group into the sweat. He said that it was so hot, there was no steam. There was no steam, yet the men in the sweat were all dripping wet from their own perspiration. When they finally came out, one of them looked at Little Bear and said, "You're not even sweating." He was not. He was as dry as when he had gone in.

Little Bear told me about a man who came to him wanting to start a sweat somewhere up in the state of Kansas. He asked Little Bear for instructions on how to go about it. Little Bear told him to draw up the plans just the way he wanted it and to prepare the ground. Then he had to take coals from Little Bear's sweat to start his fire. He had to fast and bless the ground. At last, Little Bear told him just how to prepare the medicine for pouring onto the hot rocks. The man finally got his sweat started, and when the word spread that he had gotten it from John Little Bear, people started coming to it from all around.

But there are others who just try it without knowing anything about it. Little Bear told me about another man. This one did not seek help. He thought that he already knew all about it. He decided to put up a sweat in his garage. He heated the rocks in his fireplace. He almost burned the house down.

Coming out of a properly prepared sweat run by someone who is competent to run it is first of all very refreshing. One feels cleansed and invigorated. But it can be much more than that. If a person has had bad medicine put on him or her, the sweat can help to remove it. Many people feel the need for a sweat regularly. It makes them feel good spiritually and physically. Even if they're already feeling fine, it's used as preventive medicine.

13

Going to Water

According to James Mooney (*Myths of the Cherokee*), "At times those who desired instruction from an adept in the sacred lore of the tribe met him by appointment in the asi, where they sat up all night talking, with only the light of a small fire burning in the middle of the floor. At daybreak the whole party went down to the running stream, where the pupils or the hearers of the myths stripped themselves, and were scratched upon their naked skin with a bone-tooth comb in the hands of the priest, after which they waded out, facing the rising sun, and dipped seven times under the water, while the priest recited prayers upon the bank. This purification rite, observed more than a century ago by Adair, is also part of the ceremonial of the ballplay, the Greencorn dance, and, in fact, every important ritual performance." (Mooney was writing in the 1890s, so the observation of Adair to which he refers was earlier than 1790.)

Charles Hudson, in *The Southeastern Indians*, says, "One of the principal ceremonial means of overcoming pollution in the Southeast was by bathing in creeks and rivers. . . . By overcoming pollution, bathing was believed to increase longevity."

I was sitting on the porch of Little Bear's house one afternoon, when Little Bear said to me, "I'm going to take these boys to water. You want to go along?"

At first I declined, but I quickly rethought my decision. The two brothers, Little Bear, and I got into Little Bear's big van, and Little Bear drove to a spot on Barren Fork Creek outside of Tahlequah. We all got out. Little Bear told the two young men to take off their shoes and socks and roll their trouser legs up to their knees. He then had them wade out into the cold water and turn

Going to water. Drawing by Murv Jacob.

back to face him. One of the two had not brought anything to wear on his feet out into the water, and the sharp rocks cut at his feet as he walked. He almost fell over into the creek. The rest of us laughed at him. Eventually he found a spot where he could stand more or less comfortably, and Little Bear had them both bend over and scoop up handfuls of water to throw over their heads four times. All the while, Little Bear was quietly reciting something. I was standing right beside him, and I could not hear the words. I could only see his lips move. When he was done, he called the two out of the water, and we drove back to his house. Thus, I witnessed an instance of perhaps the single most important of all Cherokee rituals. It was quiet, low key, straightforward, and matter-of-fact. Anyone looking for feathers, chanting, and dance with Native American ritual would almost certainly go away from a genuine Cherokee ritual disappointed. It's not a show. It just gets the job done.

Little Bear told me that some people can't take going into a sweat. Perhaps they have asthma or heart problems or something else that prevents them from going through a sweat. Going to the water can be used as a substitute for a sweat for those people. And sometimes, if the tobacco that was fixed for a person is not doing the job fast enough, he will take that person to the water to cleanse him or her.

14

Dreams

"Dreams are when I'm battling someone," Frank told me. "They throw things at me. Snakes. The pope."

"The pope?" I said.

Frank laughed. "Yeah. You see things that are being done or have been done. I'm fighting it. Trying to kill what they done." In one dream, Frank was standing beside a table. The pope was sitting at the opposite end. Standing off to Frank's left were three people, two female and one male. Frank looked at the pope.

"Come here, my son," the pontiff said. "Let me bless you."

Frank laughed, but he walked over to the pope.

"Kneel down, my son. Let me bless you."

Frank knelt on one knee, bowed his head, but looked up so he could watch. The pope put both hands on the back of Frank's head and pushed—hard. Frank laughed and stood up, and the pope vanished. The three people who had been standing to Frank's left were also gone.

Frank went to see Little Bear and told him this dream. Little Bear laughed heartily, and when he finished, he told Frank, "They used the pope because of his stature. They disguised their evil in religious terms."

In another dream, Frank saw Little Bear in bed at the end of a long hallway. Frank was standing in the kitchen. Little Bear called to him. Frank was hesitant for some reason, but he went on down the hall to see Little Bear. Little Bear said, "I need to doctor you for this," and he put his hand behind Frank's neck. Frank couldn't move. He was trapped. Bringing his face close to Frank's, Little Bear opened his mouth and something came out of it and went into Frank's mouth.

The next day, Frank again went to see Little Bear and told him the dream.

"What's the deal?" he asked.

Little Bear said, "It wasn't me. They were trying to suck your life out."

Little Bear said that there are different kinds of dreams, but some dreams have very specific interpretations. If you dream of a snake coming toward you, that means that someone is using medicine against you. If you dream of a snake biting you, then the medicine is already taking hold and doing its job. To dream of a deer looking directly at you is good luck. If you dream of an eagle looking at you, that means that someone is watching over you. It's also good luck. If an owl is looking at you in your dream, a medicine man is watching over you to make sure that all is well. But sometimes, he says, as in some of Frank's dreams noted above, it may not be a dream at all. It may be a shape-shifter trying to pull something on you.

15

Maggie's Story

Maggie is a Jewish woman from New Jersey, a friend of mine. While she was down in Oklahoma for a visit, I took her to meet Little Bear. She was profoundly impressed. Later, on the telephone, she told me that she was suffering from arthritis, and she was having problems with the medication they were giving her for the pain. I went to see Little Bear and asked him if he could fix something for her. Little Bear's wife gave me a bottle of liquid. The instructions were to use it like rubbing alcohol. I mailed it to Maggie. A couple of weeks later I was talking to her on the telephone again, and she said that the medicine was a great help. It was working better than anything else she had tried. What's more, she said, she had used it all through Hanukkah, and its level did not seem to be dropping in the bottle. It was another Hanukkah miracle, she said. (Following the rule of Alexander the Great, King Antiochus sent soldiers into Judea to tell the people that they must pray to his Greek gods. People in one village, known as the Maccabees, decided to fight instead. They drove the Greek soldiers out, but a long war followed. After three years, the Maccabees defeated the Greeks, but their temple was in ruins. There was not enough olive oil to keep the holy lamp burning day and night as it should. They found one small jar of oil, but it was only enough for one day, far less than what was needed for the eight days it would take them to produce more oil. They filled a lamp and made their prayers and set about gathering olives to make new oil. For the next eight days, the lamp kept burning, miraculously refilling itself. Hanukkah is called the Festival of Lights, and its celebration lasts for eight days because of this event.) Maggie has since quit using the arthritis medicine given her by her doctor, because that given her by Little Bear works so much better. She has been ordering it in great quantities, because it works so well that she has taken to giving it away to her friends who are suffering from arthritis pain.

16

Mark's Story

Mark is a former National Football League (NFL) player who was seriously down on his luck. A few years ago, he came to Tahlequah, as he put it, on a spiritual quest. While he was there, he met John Little Bear. Mark says that meeting Little Bear was like meeting a relative who had been brought up in the old ways. Little Bear had come out of the house and sat down on the porch to visit with Mark.

"How can I help you?" he asked.

Mark told him that for years things had gone bad in his life, and he couldn't figure out what was happening to him. He had financial and emotional problems. His career had come to an end. For a time, he had been homeless. Little Bear listened and occasionally asked for more information about times and places and how Mark was feeling. Mark says that just the talking seemed to help him. Saying things out loud made a difference. After a while, Little Bear told Mark, "I'm going to get to the root of all this, and we going to straighten things out." He told Mark to come back the next day and bring tobacco.

The following afternoon Little Bear sent Mark into the sweat with Frank. Mark felt relief from some of his problems while he was in the sweat. When the sweat was done, Mark was given a decoction of redroot to drink to make him vomit. When Mark was done with all of this, he went back to the porch. Little Bear was waiting inside the house. He had already "looked into" Mark's problems, and he started telling Mark what things had been put in his way and why.

"I'm going to fix what's wrong," he said.

He gave Mark back his tobacco, which had been doctored, and some redroot medicine, with instructions for their use. People trying to harm you, Little Bear said, are very unpredictable. It's hard for us to see or believe the ways in which they might be affecting our lives. Someone, in effect, had made Mark invisible. People he tried to deal with could not see him or hear what he was trying to tell them.

Mark said that as soon as he left Little Bear's yard, he could tell the difference. The positive results were immediate. Mark had been trying to meet with several local artists, and the meetings all came about. The artists showed him how to do things. Mark began to get commitments to speak to different groups, and he began using the techniques that he had learned from the artists. His whole life changed for the better.

Then came the custody battle over his little girl. The child had been born out of wedlock, and Mark and the mother had never lived together. The mother, a drug addict, had filed papers trying to make Mark pay child support. She also wanted to keep the child and thereby keep Mark in her life. Mark took the problem to Little Bear. He said that when he went to the family services people or to court, it was as if nothing he said was heard, nothing he wrote down was read and understood. Again, Little Bear told Mark to come back the next day and bring tobacco.

The next day when Mark arrived back at Little Bear's house he was put through another sweat. Following that, he was given medicine to drink to make him vomit. When he had done that, he washed himself off with the same medicine. Then he went back into the house and ate a meal prepared by Little Bear's wife. When everyone had eaten their fill, they went out onto the porch to sit and talk.

Little Bear said that he had looked into the matter. He told Mark that the people on the other side had been very busy. The mother of the child was using strong medicine, the purpose of which was to keep anything that Mark had to say from being heard. And she was using the child to keep Mark in her life. She was also using medicine to drive away Mark's present companion. He gave Mark back his tobacco, with songs in it, and told him how to make use of it. It took some time, but at last Mark won custody of his daughter in court. The little girl is now living with Mark and his partner, and they are all very happy together.

17

Rainmaker's Story

Rainmaker is half Cherokee. The rest is Irish and German. He first went to see Little Bear's grandmother after he came back from Vietnam. He was married to a full-blood Cherokee woman, and when they began having problems, his father-in-law took him to see Grandma. She gave him medicine to make the bad things go away. She told him that it wasn't something that came from inside him. Things had been put on him from outside because of the war, because of the things he had seen and done, the things that had happened to him. She gave him medicine to drink, tobacco to smoke. She gave him a coin, which he keeps hidden, but now and then, if he's having bad feelings, he takes it out and rubs it. In a day or so, the bad feelings go away.

Eventually, as Grandma got older and more tired, she told Rainmaker to go talk to her grandson, John. Rainmaker was married to a woman who was having problems with her ex-husband. But there was more. Little Bear and Frank told Rainmaker that she was nothing but trouble and that he needed to get away from her. Things got worse. Little Bear told Rainmaker that his wife was pregnant. "I ain't supposed to be able to have kids," Rainmaker said. "It ain't yours," said Little Bear. "It's time for you to get out."

Another time, Little Bear told Rainmaker to be careful. Something bad was about to happen. Rainmaker went to Tunica, Mississippi, for a few days, and when he returned, his house had burned to the ground. He went back to see Little Bear and told him about the house. "They thought you was in it," Little Bear said. "But you was gambling in Mississippi." Rainmaker had not told Little Bear about his trip to Tunica.

For a period of ten years, Rainmaker was a regular visitor, going to see Little Bear once a month. Little Bear made him a medicine bag, which he always wears; a dream catcher, which hangs on his bedroom wall; and a medicine wheel, which is hanging in his bathroom. In addition, Rainmaker went to the sweats conducted by Frank. One time Rainmaker went to a sweat in another town, and when he told Little Bear, Little Bear told him to stay away from them. "They play on the dark side," Little Bear said. "Don't go there." Rainmaker has not been back.

"He's helped me when my business has got slow," Rainmaker said. "One time I was about to lose my business." Little Bear gave him cigars to smoke, one in the morning and one at midnight. Things turned around.

Rainmaker is a biker, and once he wrecked his motorcycle. He was banged up, and he had been to several doctors, spending somewhere around $1,000. He couldn't relax. He couldn't sleep. He went to see Little Bear. Little Bear gave him some liniment. "You'll sleep tonight," he said. Rainmaker went home and rubbed the stuff all over himself and slept for two days. He made a $10 donation to Little Bear.

Rainmaker and I talked about how it's like going to the United Nations going up to Little Bear's place on a busy Saturday, there are so many different kinds of people there from all over. Rainmaker told me that Little Bear is known worldwide. He told me that he's met people in South Dakota who know him. When he was visiting in Phoenix, Arizona, one time, he met an Apache who asked him if he knew John Little Bear. When Rainmaker told him that he did know Little Bear, the Apache said, "I've never met him, but I've talked to him on the phone a number of times."

"When I first went up there," Rainmaker told me, "I didn't know if anyone would talk to me, since I'm a half-breed, but it wasn't like that. I met a lot of good people up there. I can be really depressed and go through sweats with John or with Frank and come away with a different frame of mind. I don't know how he does it, and I don't want to. That's one man I'd do anything in the world for."

18

Coby's Story

Hidden meaning

Coby is an artist. He was having some problems, and he and I were talking about it one day. I told him to go see Little Bear. He said that when I told him that Little Bear was a good medicine man, that came as a surprise. He said that usually around here you hear about how lousy a so-called medicine person is or how "they're messing with people." So Coby went up to meet Little Bear. His story was so enthusiastic and so eloquent that I decided to preserve it here almost word for word. First of all, he said that he was amazed at what he saw on his first visit, "an old ramshackle trailer in the woods, surrounded by derelict cars, trucks, vans, kids playing every place, barking dogs. There were people sitting around all over the place. There were Indian people and black people and Mexican people and some white people sitting on the porch, outside the house, in their cars, inside the house. There weren't any screens on the windows. I didn't find that unusual because I'd hung out with some traditional people up north and that's the way they were, too. Their attitude was that they'd rather live in an old crappy trailer and live their lifestyle the way they wanted to than live in some government housing where everybody told them what to do all the time and they had all that red tape to deal with.

"The people that were visiting had kind of parked off to both sides of the driveway in amongst the trees and kind of carefully so as not to block each other in. It was a Saturday in early summer, and some of these people came to do the sweat lodge ritual, some had come to talk with Little Bear, and others apparently were there just to visit but were really helping him with stuff of some sort or another.

Collection

"He would talk with people often very openly there on the porch in front of everyone, and that was kind of embarrassing to me, until I realized that we were talking about the human condition, the thing that we all find ourselves in, and the listeners were not there to gain some advantage by what was happening to me, but rather, talking about things openly like that it made it all aboveboard and made it all something that everybody could share in. We talked for a while, and then Little Bear went off to study on what we had discussed. Later, he called me into the back room of the trailer, and he told me of his revelation.

"Someone who did not like me had managed to give me a gift *Subtle* or send it along with someone else. Attached to the gift was a kind of a sgili, or a monster of some sort, that once it got inside of my art studio, unfolded itself and manifested itself, and it had been at work on me for quite a while. I'd had problems, and I knew that the middle room of the studio, when you'd walk in there you could feel a cold chill sometimes even in the summertime. I mean just the hair would stand up on the back of your neck. I had a couple of ferrets that lived in the studio, and within a couple of months both of these ferrets had become sick and died mysteriously. There wasn't any apparent cause of death for either of them. Both of them ended up having to go into the vet— dead.

"Little Bear said that this thing was trying to do several things to me. It was trying to sew shut my eyes so I couldn't see. It was trying to sew shut my ears so I couldn't hear what people were saying to me. And it was trying to sew shut my mouth so I couldn't communicate with people I was trying to converse with. People just wouldn't pay any attention to what I was trying to say. It made sense to me. Things had been really a jumble. Things were just a mess. We had the most awful person you could imagine who had just become chief. And I had at that point become sort of a nonentity around here. I had been doing pretty well, and then that series of books with Doubleday had kind of folded up on me. I was just pretty much not doing anything. It was a bad period. It was a real dark time. Even though it sounded fantastic, what he was saying, somehow it rang of truth, that somehow they were able to use that old medicine and do this to me. Somebody probably paid them do it. I think we know who's involved, and he's still around, and Little Bear won't say.

"For years I had been at war with those art law people. I'm an Indian artist without tribal membership, and they had fought both openly and secretly to destroy me. And for a long time people had been warning me that people were doing medicine on me. They'd heard it from different medicine men. I was getting calls. Little Bear said I needed to take a series of medicinal sweats by myself, or with just me and the doctor, and he had Frank running it and George helping him. I had to go through four sweats. He told me that if I thought those people were doing medicine on me I should not sock them in the teeth or sock them in the eye, which is my first nature. But I should let him handle it on a higher level. So I agreed to do that, and I haven't threatened those people anymore, or beat them up anymore, or anything like that. I let him handle it.

"But then we started talking, and he decided that he needed to come over here and smoke this place, the art studio. And they showed up in that old van outside, and he had Frank with him, and Frank built a fire in a gallon can, and he had Sally with him, and he didn't even get out of the van that day. He sat there in the van, and he had some herbs and stuff, and he put them all in a bag, and then it seemed like he was talking and blowing smoke into the bag. He had that gallon can with a wire handle on it, and he put some charcoal down in the bottom of it and some cedar, and burned it, and then they put the medicine down in there.

"Frank and Sally went all around the art studio. It seems like she had some kind of a little fan or something she was using. They went all around the art studio, and they opened up both the doors. You know, this place runs east and west, and they opened up both doors, and they smoked every room and every corner of every room, and when they finally got done, they went back outside, and Little Bear got out of the van, and he was sitting there talking to them. He said, 'Well, what was it?' and Sally said, 'It was in that middle room, and it looked like some kind of a green bug,' and she said, 'It flew around me three times, and then it went out that east door, and it's gone now,' and Little Bear said, 'Doctor up some cedar to put by the back door, and doctor up that tobacco that he's got by his front door, so that nothing can come into that place anymore to bother him,' and he said, 'From now on, nothing's going to come in this place unless you want it in here,' and I've noticed that for the last two or three years, people will come up and try my door, and that door will be locked, only that door is not locked. That door just doesn't want to let those people in. The door's like an extension of me now. Now there's not someone else running things here anymore. And it's really an extension of him. He sits up there on that mountain. If you walk out in the middle of the street in front of the studio, you can look right down that the street up to that mountain where he lives and see it up there, and its almost like he can look right down the street into this place. I mean it really feels like that. It feels like that while we're talking right now, doesn't it? He's laying over there sleeping on that hill, but he's seeing everything that's going on here. And he said, he explained to me that thing shouldn't be able to come back in here and bother anybody again, and it's been a totally different place ever since then.

"And now when I go up there to sweat, I just go in with everyone else. It's pretty good. I've gotten cigarettes that he's doctored from him. He told me to just smoke one in the evening and take that smoke and kind of rub it around on me. I go through a couple or three packs of cigarettes every two or three months because I consider them to be a real powerful talisman, and now when I go up there, he asks me, 'What do you want these to do?' and I say, 'I really don't have any problems, but I just don't have much money now,' and he says, 'Well, you want some medicine to make you lucky or make the money come to you?' and I say, 'Sure, but more than that, just make things happen.' I want some of that stuff that when I smoke it, it just stirs things up. You don't know what's going to happen. It's going to be something. This is a small town. There isn't much going on. I'd like some tobacco that just really stirs things up and makes it interesting. I want to go sit on the porch of that café over there and smoke one of those cigarettes and see who shows up and what the conversation is, where it goes and what happens. That's how I use it now. I just kind of use it as a catalyst to kind of stir up the beans, see what kind of pops up out of there. I haven't really had any big problems since I been going to him. There's an old Chinese curse that says may you live in interesting times. Well, these times aren't that interesting. I need some of his tobacco to kind of stir things up and make them a little more interesting."

19

James's Story

James went to see Little Bear with all kinds of problems. He had been fussing with his wife. His friends had quit coming around. He was getting into arguments regularly with his neighbors on both sides. He was unable to concentrate on anything. Little Bear asked him if anyone had been in his yard. James said, yes, the neighbors had been crossing it lately. Little Bear fixed some medicine from redroot for James to use in his yard, and James poured it on his yard and smoked cigarettes that Little Bear had fixed for him.

Then James and his wife and son all started hearing scratching on their windows at night. If James went outside to investigate, there was nothing to be seen. Back inside, the scratching continued. One day James saw a copperhead on his front porch. He went after something to kill it with, but when he came back it was gone. He saw it again later, and the same thing happened. The third time it went under the porch. James took a can of charcoal lighter fluid and poured it through he cracks around the porch. He considered lighting it but thought better of it. He never saw it again, but he did go to see Little Bear.

"They're mad because you're fighting back," Little Bear said. "We got a fight on our hands."

James became sick to his stomach. His left leg turned black with infection and developed a thick skin. He was afraid that he would lose the leg, and he is still convinced that he came close to dying. His head hurt. He said that it felt like something was pressing on his head from behind. At last, he went to see Little Bear again.

He kept smoking the doctored cigarettes for a month. No matter how late he stayed up, he would wake up at six o'clock every morning. That was the time he was supposed to smoke the medicine. Things at last began to calm down. James was also going to the sweats. His head felt better. Little Bear said that the neighbors had been dropping some kind of medicine in the yard when they cut across it. Then one day, James found a feather in his pickup, inside the camper shell on the back. He also found an owl feather inside his house. He went to see Little Bear again, and Little Bear went back to work on the problem. The neighbor on one side lost his white pickup shortly after James got one for himself. The financing came easy to him. He asked Little Bear what was going on. "He was stealing things from you," Little Bear said.

Then one day James met an Indian woman with car problems. He tried to fix the car for her but was unable to. He told her about a place in Tahlequah where she could get a car. She said she was waiting for her husband to get out of prison. A short time later, she came to James's house. She told him that her father-in-law had died. "They think there's foul play involved," she said. "They found him naked on his front porch. He was all beat up." James wondered why she had told him that. He asked her if she still wanted to go after a car. She did, but she was still waiting for her husband. Later she came back, and her husband was with her. He was wearing dark glasses, and he wouldn't look at James. He told James the same story about his father.

James brought them to Tahlequah to get a car. They got a car and went on their way. James went up to see Little Bear. He told him what these people had told him. Little Bear already knew. He smiled. "We got him," he said.

"What do you mean?" James asked.

Little Bear told him that the old man was the medicine man who had been working against him. He was naked because he had been flying around in another shape, a crow or an owl or something. He had been changed back to his normal shape while he was in the air, and, as a result, he had fallen to his death. That was the explanation for the battered shape his old body was found in.

James felt bad for the old man on hearing that, but Little Bear told him that he was not responsible for what had happened. He said that he had met the old man and told him to quit bothering James. He had refused to listen to reason, so Little Bear had been forced "to put him down." When a man suffers, even dies, from using bad medicine, it is because the bad medicine has been turned back around on him. In fact, he has killed himself with the medicine he made to bring harm to someone else. It's as if he threw a baseball against a wall, and it bounced back to strike him.

"How come I met that woman, and how come they came to tell me what happened to the old man?"

"It's like a rule," said Little Bear. "When something like this happens, the family has to come to you and tell you about it."

When James calmed down, he told Little Bear that he had gone to other medicine men in the past but to no avail. He asked why they had not been able to help him. "Well, they just weren't strong enough," Little Bear said. "You had some kind of a block on you, and I know how to deal with it. Maybe they didn't know how, or maybe they just didn't want to."

The worst was over, but James was still having problems with his neighbors. On one side were white people. Little Bear fixed some medicine to make them move away. He told James to throw it on their porch and to be careful not to get any of it on himself. "When you've scattered it," he said, "drop the bag. Go to the river and wash your hands and your shoes." He told James not to touch his car because it would tear his car up. James got a friend to help. He was so mad at the white neighbors that he went over to their house in broad daylight and threw the medicine on the porch. The boys in the family came out and walked in the medicine. This family had been there in the same location for ten years. One month later they moved out of town.

Later, when James was out hunting, he came across a deer carcass in his path. He drug it off in the ditch. The next day he went out hunting again and found it back in the same spot. Again, he went to see Little Bear. Little Bear told him to go back to the same spot, shoot an arrow into the carcass, and tell it to go back where it came from. James did what he was told to do. Nothing has ever come of the deer carcass.

When all of his troubles were over and done, James was visiting with Little Bear late one night. It was deer season, and all of a sudden, Little Bear asked, "You got your rifle out in the car?"

"Yeah," said James.

"Is it loaded?"

"Yeah."

"Go get it and go out there by the sweat. There's a deer out there. Go kill it."

"How do you know there's a deer out there?" James asked, incredulous.

"Never mind that," said Little Bear. "Just go shoot it."

Little Bear told one of his daughters to go along and carry a light. James and the girl went outside. The girl carried a light, and James got his rifle out of the car. Then they walked out to the sweat lodge. A good-sized buck was standing twenty yards away. James took aim and fired. The buck jerked, ran, and fell down just beside the sweat lodge. James went over to look at it and discovered that its left leg was a mass of infection. He cut it off and threw it away, cleaning and cutting up the rest. The meat went in Little Bear's freezer. No explanation was ever offered.

20

Laura's Story

The following is in Laura's own words.

EXPERIENCES WITH JOHN LITTLE BEAR

"I am a friend and clan relative of John Little Bear. I have gone to him for help for a number of years. I am a Navajo and Cherokee woman, living on the Navajo Reservation, and I use traditional healers from both tribal traditions. I have apprenticed with and learned from crystals (diagnosticians) from both traditions.

"There are some overall similarities between the two traditions of healing, but each tribe has its own specific methods and herbs, tied closely to the land and to the traditional language. In the Navajo way, one has a healing ceremony and goes forward with a definite belief and faith that the healing has been initiated and will happen. You are not supposed to talk about the healing procedure after it has been done. You just act as if your healing is complete.

"In the Cherokee way, however, you can talk about the healing process, and since John Little Bear and the patient both gave me permission, I will tell a story about one specific healing in which I participated.

"A close friend of mine works for the Navajo Nation government and is a traditional Navajo medicine man. He is a Vietnam veteran and lives on the western side of the Navajo Reservation, close to Tuba City, Arizona. Eddie Begay has had numerous traditional ceremonies done, including ones to mitigate the effects of wartime combat. He has a reoccurring leg injury that causes him great pain and dangerous infections in the blood stream.

"On this occasion he became very ill with a fever that came on fast and quickly rose to a dangerous level. He became almost delirious and was in great pain. He was sent in an ambulance to the Tuba City Hospital, where he was tested and eventually given strong antibiotics. However, the infection had taken a hold of him, and although he had stabilized, he was not getting any better.

"I visited Eddie in the hospital and was alarmed by his condition. His leg was greatly swollen and excruciatingly painful. His normally brown skin was a bright angry red from his foot to his knee. Nothing the doctors had done was helping his leg to heal.

"I called out to Oklahoma and spoke with John Little Bear. He said he would 'check things out' and get back to me in a few hours. When I next spoke with him he said Eddie's bad leg was caused by witchcraft, and if we didn't act fast it would take his life. He told me to gather certain parts from a plant which grows out here (datura) and to boil them until the water turned dark. The solution would need to be applied to Eddie's leg as soon as possible.

"I drove several hours to a place where I knew the datura plant grows. I found the plant and prayed to it in a traditional way, in Navajo, asking the plant's help in healing Eddie. I asked permission of the plant to use its leaves and roots for a healing purpose. Then I collected what I needed and returned home. I prepared the plant as I had been instructed, mashing the roots and boiling them until the water was dark, and took the infusion to the hospital. I had to sneak in after hours, as this kind of healing was not part of regular hospital protocol.

"We applied the darkish liquid to Eddie's leg, and I returned home. Eddie is not Cherokee, but he has faith in different Native traditions. In the middle of the night he woke up to the beat of wings at his window. He could just make out the form of a huge eagle outside his room. Amazingly, he felt relaxed and went back to sleep almost immediately.

"In the morning I called him to see how he was doing. He was cheerful and optimistic. He told me that his leg was less painful and that the swelling was going down. The fierce red color was fading to dark pink. He told me about the visit of the eagle. I called

John Little Bear and told him the news. John just chuckled, his deep confident chuckle, when I asked him if the eagle was him. I know that he is a shape-shifter and travels and does his work at night.

"Eddie continued to improve, and his recovery astounded the doctors. Of course, we never told them what had really occurred. Some months later, a fully recovered Eddie and I traveled to Oklahoma to thank John. We took him datura roots and mountain tobacco. We talked about long-distance healing and the power of spirit.

"I am honored to have a friend and healer such as John Little Bear. His knowledge and spiritual powers are truly awesome. His work lies in a cosmic area, little known and seldom understood by the medical establishment. Hundreds and maybe even thousands of people have been helped by him. I have many other stories about his healing powers and his help for me and for my children, for my mother and other relatives. But this is enough for now."

21

Indian Medicine and Christianity

Over the years I have heard a great many Indian people argue against one side or the other on whether Christianity conflicts with Indian religion. I have heard "traditional" people disparage the church and make fun of Indians who go to church and follow "the white man's religion." On the other hand, I have heard many church-going Indians say that the devil is at the stomp ground, and Indian medicine is the devil's work. I have heard Frank talk about the Bible, and I noticed that when John Little Bear's grand-mother died, there was a Christian preacher at the funeral. So I asked Little Bear, how do you reconcile Christianity and Indian medicine?

He told me that medicine was given to us a long time ago by the Great Spirit, and that's the same as God. "Every time I make medicine," he said, "I pray over it." The stomp ground is a church without walls, he said. At a stomp dance, there will be several medicine men watching over everyone. Before anyone goes into the dance circle, he or she must be purified. Little Bear sees no conflict between traditional ways and Christianity. Different people just try different ways, he said. He does think, though, that for Indians, it's better to raise children in the ways of their ancestors. Sometimes you hear people talk against the stomp ground or Indian medicine, he said. They think it's not right, but where do they think it came from? It came from God.

Syncretism

22

The Little People

I was over visiting John Little Bear one afternoon, and we were sitting on the front porch. Little Bear was looking for something. He called it by its name, but I don't recall now what it was. What I do remember was that Little Bear frowned and said, "Those dag-gone Little People. They're always hiding things from me." He mentioned a couple of other items they had moved from their proper places. I had heard before and read somewhere that the Little People liked to hang around Cherokee medicine men. They helped them in their work, but they were also mischievous, liking especially to hide things from the medicine man. One of the other things I had heard about them was that they look after children in the woods. Also, if you find something in the woods, say, a knife, it's really theirs, and when you pick it up, you're supposed to say to the Little People, "Little People, I'm taking this knife." I think you're supposed to leave them something in return for it, say a bit of tobacco or something. Anyhow, Little Bear went on to say, on the occasion mentioned above, that he had put out some of my whiskey for them, and they really liked it. He said that they like the honeycomb from a jar of local honey. I asked him if he would tell me about them, and he said the next time I came out, he would.

I finally got the chance to ask Little Bear to tell me some more about the Little People. He said that there are certain songs he uses to call them up. "We use them to do things," he said. "We ask them for help and send them places to do things." They might be asked to protect people in their homes. Some unscrupulous peo-ple use bad medicine on old people, Little Bear told me. "We ask the Little People to help take care of the old people." Like with anyone else, he told me, among the Little People there are mean ones and good ones. They can turn a person crazy, or "they can go after a real pretty woman for you."

23

Corrine's Story

Corrine got some medicine from Little Bear because she felt like she was under siege at work. There were people who were messing with her on a daily basis. She felt like they were using medicine against her, and she felt like the only way she could protect herself from what they were doing was to have some medicine of her own. So Little Bear fixed her up a thing that she keeps with her all the time, and she's got another thing that she keeps underneath her bed where she sleeps. She's got some of his medicine there to protect her. There are animals where Corrine works, and at that time, a number of those animals were dying, and a horse kept getting out. When it would come back or when they would find it, it would be all torn up. They said it was lightning that hit those animals, but the animals were literally torn to pieces, and, as Corrine said, "They don't send a detective out there when animals get killed." All the animals out there were killed: sheep, goats. All but the horse, and the horse was all torn up. Bloody. It was a mess out there for a while. There was something going on all the time.

When the power was off one time out there, Corrine and her husband went out to retrieve some stuff out of her basement office. They were about halfway across the parking lot when they heard a most awful sound, they told me. "It sounded like somebody sawing through metal with a power saw. We could see there was something down in there," they went on, "but it didn't seem real to either of us. It looked like a black shadow just moving down there from tree to tree. Around that place."

They left, and later they went up to see Little Bear. He fixed some medicine for Corrine, and she keeps it with her all the time.

Her worst enemy at work was coming down the stairs one day after that, and Corrine looked at her, and she told me, "I could see it in her eyes that she wished I would fall down those stairs, and right then she fell down the stairs and fell all the way to the bottom. She went away after that, and she never came back." Her other enemy insisted on having things out at a meeting, and every time he would start in on her, she'd just reach inside her pocket and rub that medicine she carried, and he would just fall back, and he'd start crying. He would get very emotional and start screaming. "It was unbelievable," Corrine said. "Every time he'd start on me, I'd rub that medicine, and every time I'd rub, he would just fall back down. It was like kryptonite to the guy. He just couldn't stand up." Finally, she got everything resolved with him. He's kept his job, but Corrine hasn't had any more trouble with him. "He hasn't done a thing since then," she said.

24

Agnes's Story

Agnes told me that she had only known Little Bear for about a year, but in that time he had done a great deal of good for her and her family. She had a seventeen-year-old son who was always giving them trouble. Little Bear doctored him and calmed him down, even keeping him out of prison. Now, she said, they always know where the boy is. He comes in at reasonable hours, and he acts like he cares.

Someone was trying to break up her family. They were about to split her and her husband apart. Again, Little Bear doctored them. He put them through the sweat and got rid of all the bad stuff that was on them. Agnes said that she would get depressed, and she had called and talked to Sally, telling her that she was thinking about getting a divorce. Sally told her not to do that, to come and see them. She did, and then everything was all right.

Little Bear finally discovered that it was her ex-husband behind all the trouble they'd been having. He tried to make them lose everything they had. He was causing their other son to have problems with his girlfriend and to think that everything was his fault. Little Bear helped him to see things more clearly. A daughter was also having trouble with her husband. Little Bear and Sally went to her house and doctored the house. The couple is now doing all right. They stayed together.

Another daughter had a bad fever, and nothing the doctors did was helping. At last, the parents took her to see Little Bear. He doctored the girl with redroot, and the fever broke before they had even driven back home.

Agnes told me that there had been times when she had problems and no money, but Little Bear had told her to come and see him anyway. Her husband is a firefighter who is sometimes away from home for extended periods of time. Little Bear and Sally told her that if she ever needed anything while he was away, groceries or anything else, to let them know. They'd take care of her. "If it wasn't for Little Bear and Sally," she said, "my whole family would be all split up."

25

Emiliano's Story

Emiliano went to see Little Bear on someone's recommendation. His problem was that all he had ever wanted to do was play soccer. He had played in college, and he knew that he was as good as any of them, but no one with the professional teams would give him a contract. He had tried out with all of them. In some cases, he had played for a week or so with a team and then been cut loose. One time a team in Mexico had actually offered him a contract, only to discover that he was not a Mexican citizen but a citizen of the United States. (His father is Mexican, but his mother is a Cherokee, and he was born in the United States.) This particular team will not hire foreigners. Emiliano had even been to Europe to try out with soccer teams. He had never before been to see a medicine man and was very unsure of what was expected of him. Little Bear went off to read on him, while I stayed on the porch and visited with the young man.

When he returned, Little Bear said that there had been another young man who wanted to play soccer in college, but Emiliano was always better than he was. This young man's grandfather had doctored Emiliano in such a way that no one could see him. No one would pay any attention to him. No one would give him a contract.

Little Bear said, "I know you don't want to smoke." But he told him that he could come to the sweats. He told him to come around the next Saturday and go through twice. Then come two weeks later and go through twice again. That would take off all the bad medicine. Within a month, Little Bear said, Emiliano would have a contract. Since then, the young man has enrolled in the University of Tulsa in order to play soccer. This story is ongoing.

26

Jeff's Story

Jeff is a young man, half Cherokee and half Cheyenne, but he grew up out west with the Cheyennes, his mother's people. He went to school at the American Indian Arts Institute in Santa Fe, New Mexico. When he returned home to western Oklahoma, he began to sell his artwork, and he was doing fairly well at it. He told me that it had been about the middle of July (only about three months before our conversation) when his nephew had stopped by the house and asked him to drive him somewhere. Jeff said that he never refuses his nephew, so he agreed.

"Where do you want to go?" he asked.

"Arizona," the nephew answered.

"All right."

They drove to Arizona and stayed for a week. Then they headed back for Oklahoma. They stopped in Albuquerque, New Mexico, and then they went to the Navajo Reservation. Jeff felt like something wasn't right. They went to someplace south of Shiprock, and then they went to Gallup. Jeff continued to feel out of place. They were staying with some people there, and the first night, Jeff said, "Something ran down the street and back three or four times." Dogs were barking all the way. At first, he thought it was just another dog running. He asked them to close the windows, and they did.

The next day, they were sitting around outside talking and playing dice. Someone started talking about Skinwalkers. "How do they do it?" someone asked.

"I don't know."

"Well, don't worry about it. We're protected."

But that night, the same thing happened again. When Jeff asked for the window to be closed, the woman of the house said that it was too hot. "Well, put the blinds down," he said. As she moved to put down the blinds, Jeff saw something white go by the window. He said that it was like someone wrapped in a sheet. Just then, the Rottweiler they had outside started barking like he was going crazy. Eventually, Jeff went on to sleep, but in the middle of the night, his nephew jerked the sheet off him, waking him up.

"What the hell?" Jeff shouted.

The next day his nephew told him, "Something was playing with my hair," and the nephew's wife said the same thing. Then Jeff said that something kept telling him to go get a beer. He knew that something was wrong. At last, they drove on back home.

Reaching home, Jeff discovered that his father had been in an automobile wreck, and his mother's face had dropped on one side. Jeff was broke. The sales of his artwork had dropped off to nothing, and it seemed as if nothing was going to change. Nothing would come. Things just kept getting worse. He started drinking beer, smoking marijuana, smoking crack, and popping pills. Then he had a wreck. He was sitting at home. He had just about given up. He was looking at a bottle of sleeping pills and thinking about taking them all.

His father came in just at the right time and suggested that they go to the lake. They did, and Jeff was looking at the cottonwood trees and the willows that grew there. He recalled that in the Cheyenne ceremonies, they used cottonwood and willow, and he started to pray. An old school chum popped into his head. Later, back home, the same old chum actually dropped by. Jeff told him all about his trip west and the things that had been happening. "That's the way they do," the chum said. "Someone might be after you or someone close to you, but paths cross. You get caught in it."

Jeff felt a little better, but he went to visit a relative, who told him, "Those people set traps for you. They want something bad to happen to you." Jeff went to see a Cheyenne medicine person who "smoked him off," and he began to feel better, but his nephew was off somewhere in trouble.

Jeff's Cherokee father, however, wanted to make sure that everything would be all right. He suggested that they go to the Cherokee side, and he asked another Cherokee relative, who suggested they go to see John Little Bear. They drove the distance to Little Bear's home, and Jeff told him this tale.

Little Bear checked on it. He told Jeff, "Someone put a curtain in front of your face. You don't have your own thoughts." Jeff said that expressed it perfectly. "It was like something took over my head," he said. Little Bear fixed them some medicine. Everything is better now. The nephew is back home. Jeff is no longer drinking and using drugs. Things are going well. Little Bear, he said, "fixed it all up."

27

Chris's Journey

I met Chris one afternoon at Little Bear's home, and Little Bear introduced us and asked Chris if he would mind telling me his story. He told me that Chris had gone through some particularly hard times. Chris was ready to tell his tale. He sat beside me and started to talk. He first met Little Bear, he said, in 1999. He had bad drug and alcohol problems, as well as post-traumatic stress disorder (PTSD). He had been in and out of Veterans Administration (VA) hospitals, and they had not helped him. He was suffering from stress, and he had hallucinations and flashbacks. He was allergic to all the medicine they gave him, and he developed hepatitis C in the hospital. His job had "gone to hell." He no longer cared about life or anything. Three of his old friends had died of alcoholism. He tried to kill himself, stabbing himself in the belly, slashing his throat, and slashing at his chest. He survived it all. He asked God, "Why did you take my friends? They wanted to live and keep on drinking. I wanted to die and tried to kill myself, and it didn't work."

At last, Chris's father took him to see Little Bear. Little Bear and Sally talked to him. He says they told him just a little at a time. "Be humble, to yourself, to the creator. Things will start working out." Little Bear sent him through the sweats and gave him medicine. It was slow, partly because, Chris says, he would take Little Bear's medicine and then he would drink. At last, it seemed to work. He told me, "Little Bear and Sally will spank you good." His whole life has turned around. He no longer has a craving for alcohol. The hepatitis C is almost gone. He has not smoked pot for three months and has not used cocaine for six months. The smell of alcohol makes him sick. He no longer takes any medicine the VA gave him. He takes only the medicine he gets from Little Bear.

Now, he told me, he sees things in a positive way. "If I was still at the VA," he said, "I'd be dead." In fact, in May (he told me in November) they had given him one hour to live. That hour has stretched into six months. Driving home one day, he told his father, "Look at that kite." Then he realized that it was not a kite. They stopped the car and got out and saw that it was a large bird, brownish with white underneath. From the description, it sounded like he had seen an eagle. He was driving in Oklahoma City. He believes that it was a sign of good luck coming. In Oklahoma City, he said, "I'm happy to see a turtle on the road."

Chris has been reading the Bible, and like Little Bear, he sees no contradictions or conflicts with the Native ways. When he listens to a Christian preacher find conflicts, he says the man just hasn't read the right parts of the Bible. One evening he was at home waiting for his father to come home from church, and suddenly the house brightened up, "like a big bright spirit." He thought he was seeing things, but when his father arrived, he saw it, too. Little Bear has told Chris to tell his story to others, particularly to young people, to let them know where drugs and alcohol can lead and to let them know that if they should stray, there is a way back.

28

James Again

James said that all he ever really wanted was a nice home. He and his wife have one son who is about twelve years old. They had knocked around for several years, and the best they had ever done was to get into a low-rent Cherokee Nation apartment complex. James went to see Little Bear with this problem. He told him that he did not want to get rich. He just wanted a home, but his credit rating was lousy. Little Bear made him some medicine in the form of cigarettes and told him how and when to use them. "You'll see those numbers go up," Little Bear said. James used them faithfully and religiously. He got a credit card. Then another. His wife, who had her own separate credit rating that had been better than James's all along, could not get a credit card. James wound up with a whole mess of credit cards. He went to the bank for a small loan, and the woman at the bank looked up his credit rating, and she said that she did not understand it. It should not have been so good, but the numbers were right there in front of her. James finally had to back off of his credit cards. He was about to get himself into trouble with them. But just recently he was approved for a new Cherokee home. It's not a giveaway. His house payments are over $500 a month. It's a nice home, and the family has now moved into it. James and his wife are both working at good jobs, so they can make their payments, and James is just about as happy as he can be. He has what he most wanted.

29

Miscellaneous Tales and Anecdotes

THE RED HEN

One time, some years back, Little Bear had been out running around with a friend. They had driven to Cookson, several miles away. It was around midnight, and they were returning to the home of Little Bear's grandmother. They saw a red hen walking toward the house. What was a hen doing out that time of night? It was Grandma.

THE MISSING HUSBAND

There was a Mexican living in Fort Smith with his wife and young son. The wife came to see Little Bear in tears. The husband had left them and gone back to Mexico. She had no job, no money, no way to take care of herself and her eight-year-old son. She wanted her husband to come back to them. He had been gone for a month. Little Bear fixed her some medicine and told her, "He'll be back soon." One week later, the son telephoned Little Bear and said, "My daddy's back."

THE VANISHING TUMOR

Some people brought a man to see Little Bear because he had a tumor on his brain. The doctors had told the man that there was no hope. There was nothing more they could do. Little Bear doctored him. He took him through the sweat twice. The man had yet another appointment with his doctor at the hospital, and Little Bear told him to keep that appointment. "They ain't going to find no tumor," he told the man. The man kept the appointment, and they found no tumor. That happened eight or nine years ago, and the man is still alive and is still working. There is still no sign of a tumor.

THE BANK LOAN

Little Bear recently went to the bank to borrow $12,000. He used four cigarettes, and he got the money.

THE BAR

Some people own a bar outside of Tahlequah. They had been doing good business, but one day the police came in and told everyone to get out. The next night, a buzzard landed on the roof. After that there were no customers. Finally, the owners went to see Little Bear. He went to the bar to doctor it. The customers started coming back. He has gone back again and again, and each time he goes to the bar, their business improves.

THE PAIR OF SHOES

A woman had a married daughter who had moved to California with her husband. After she became pregnant, she started having problems with her husband and, like so many young people, ran back home to her mother. The mother went to see Little Bear. He told her to bring him a pair of her daughter's shoes. When she came back with the shoes, Little Bear doctored them and gave them back to the mother. He told her to take them home and place them on the floor, pointed west. Soon after, the daughter went back to California to her husband. Everything is all right with them now.

LUCK

Marvin and Gertie often go to Arkansas to dig for crystals. Recently they made such a trip, but before launching into the project, they smoked a cigarette Little Bear had doctored for them for luck. They went on about the business of digging, and they had a very good day. They weren't ready to quit, but they decided to take a break and go find a telephone to call home on and check on their children. They drove down the road and found a gas station, closed, but there was a phone booth there, so they stopped. There was nothing else in sight, no people around. Gertie went into the phone booth to make the call and found a $20 bill on the floor. They looked around and found another and another and a five for a total of $65.

THE "WANABEE"

There is a "wanabee" medicine man in town who put some people up to calling John Little Bear. They said that this phony was using medicine against them, and they wanted Little Bear to make some medicine for them to counter it. He checked into it and found them out for what they were. When they called back, he told them that he couldn't help them for another week. He had seen that they were trying to get some medicine from him to take to the other man, so that he could examine it and try to find out what it was that Little Bear was using. He wanted to steal Little Bear's medicine.

THE PREDICTION

James was visiting with Little Bear one day. He mentioned that his wife was worried because her grandmother was in the hospital. Little Bear told James to give him a half an hour. He went back into his room to check things out. When he came back, he said, "She's going this time." He told James that his wife's grandmother would leave them on Saturday night, really Sunday morning, at about two o'clock. James went home and told his wife that she had better go visit her grandmother. He told her what Little Bear had said. The wife had a good cry, then went to visit her grandmother and say her good-byes. Early the following Sunday morning, about two o'clock, the old woman died.

ROBERT J. CONLEY

GUNFIGHTERS

Once John Little Bear got into a "fight" with an old medicine man. Sometimes, Little Bear tells me, it's like two old gunfighters going after each other just to see who is the best. That is apparently what was happening. The man just wanted to test Little Bear's power, his medicine. When Little Bear sent his own medicine back after the man, the man would go under water. He would come up someplace else. The medicine kept missing him. At last, Little Bear used a mirror to catch him. He won the fight, bringing the other man "way down." Then Little Bear let him go, and they became fast friends. They even work together sometimes to find a cure for someone. He told me about another one who tried to get him. This one was a Creek. Little Bear whipped him good, and the man started teaching him some things about Creek medicine. "Any time you need some help," he said, "just call on me."

HOT ENOUGH?

A man Little Bear had dragged out of the gutter a while back came around for the sweat. For some reason, he had turned against Little Bear, and his intention was to mess up the sweat. He brought a friend along to help him. Frank figured them out right away, and he took them in the sweat without anyone else. He made the sweat extra hot. One of the two lasted for only about ten minutes. The other one was almost on the floor.

"Have you had enough?" Frank asked him.

"I can take it," the man said.

"Bring me some more rocks," Frank called out to his assistant. The man said, "I've had enough," and he left the sweat.

THE AILING MEDICINE MAN

Things got real busy, and someone was after one of the medicine men Little Bear works with. The medicine man was not watching his back, and Little Bear was so busy that he wasn't watching either. Little Bear's associate got sick. Then Little Bear's wife, Sally, got sick and had to be put in the hospital. That made Little Bear mad, and he really went to work on the problem in earnest. Now his associate is all right, Sally is all right, and the medicine man who was working against them is ailing considerably.

THE CHEYENNE VISITOR

We were sitting on the porch visiting, Little Bear, a visiting Cheyenne, and me. The Cheyenne asked Little Bear if he had ever seen a Bigfoot. Little Bear told us that one time he had been driving somewhere along a lonely road, and he saw something big that seemed to be whittling, sitting alone beside the road. He stopped and backed up slowly, and he saw that it was a Bigfoot. The thing saw him, got up, and calmly walked away.

The Cheyenne said that he had been out being rowdy with some other kids one time, and they thought that they saw one. They stopped their car on a bridge. Someone challenged one of the bunch to get out and holler at it, and he did. The one telling the story then said that he looked over the edge of the bridge and saw it there looking up at them. They drove away as fast as they could.

He said there were lots of old stories among the Cheyennes about being out on a buffalo hunt and seeing one of them straighten up and look around. It was a Bigfoot, traveling with the buffalo herds.

Little Bear said that there are Bigfoot songs to be used if one is about to get into a fight. Then he said that someone a few years ago had gone to the local county sheriff to report having seen a Bigfoot on the "mountain" outside of Tahlequah. When he gave the location, the sheriff laughed. "Hell, that was just ole John Little Bear that you saw up there," he said.

THE STRANGEST EXPERIENCE

Little Bear told me that for about a year, he had been feeling that something was missing from his life. He would get angry for no reason. Then a young woman showed up and told him her mother's name. The mother was a woman that Little Bear had "gone out with" in California some years ago, about the time the young woman had been born. They compared notes and discovered that Little Bear was in fact her father. She was not close to the "father" she had grown up with. The discovery having been made, she almost immediately fit into the family. Little Bear says, "She walks like me, and she talks like me. When she gets mad, I get mad, even if she's in another town." For someone whose life has been packed with strange experiences, Little Bear says that this has been the strangest of all.

SLOW RECOVERY

There was a family with a good home. The husband had been working at the same job for thirteen years and worked himself up to the position of a supervisor. The wife also had a good job. For some reason, the wife began having trouble at her job, and she went to John Little Bear for help. He helped her, and he told her to change jobs. She did. Then one day her husband came home and told her that he had quit his job—for no reason. He wasn't even sure why he had quit. Soon after that, the wife lost her new job. They lost their home. She has been seeing Little Bear for help again, and she has a temporary job and good prospects for a permanent job. Little Bear is continuing to work with them.

THE BASKETBALL STAR

A young Indian woman came to Little Bear for help. She was going to college on a basketball scholarship and doing fairly well, but she was afraid of the crowds. That was puzzling, because in high school she had been, in fact, "a star," and she had enjoyed the attention of the crowds. Another college had recruited her away from her first school. At that point, someone apparently became jealous of her. She was walking on the campus one day, and a young Indian man walking by her told her that she was nothing. Things started getting bad for her. Eventually, she says, she "went crazy." At a party one evening, she says, someone put something into her drink. She began hallucinating, and one evening she was on her porch screaming. She was taken away to an institution where she was treated for two years. When she first entered the place, she was given a blood test, and there were traces of heroin and morphine in her blood. She had never used either, she said. One of the workers in the institution told her one day, "In high school you were a star, but you're in here now, and you're nothing." Her mother went to Little Bear for help, and he began working on her behalf. One day, the young woman says, it was as if a veil was lifted from her face. Her mind was clear. She wondered where she was though. She talked to her mother, who told her what all had happened and what all Little Bear had done for her. She's gone through the sweats, and Little Bear has taken her to water. Today she is back in school, back on a basketball scholarship and doing very well. She is writing a book about her life and all her troubles. And she says she wants to go back home in a limousine to the town where she played basketball and let everyone see that she is doing well. She wants to go dancing—sober. In the past, she says, she thought that she had to be drunk to dance. She's doing fine now, she says, with Little Bear helping her. She said, "It's as if I died, and this is the real me."

A JEALOUS SISTER

Little Bear helped a man who kept losing one job after another. When he finally had the man all fixed up, things began to start happening to the man's daughter. She was a track star, but all of a sudden, something went wrong with her legs. Little Bear worked with her and fixed her legs so she could run again. In college, she was majoring in psychology, but then something went wrong with her head. She would study for a test and know it all, then the next day take the test and write down something other than what she was thinking. She knew the material, yet it came out totally different on a test. Little Bear is currently working on that with her. When he looked into all the trouble this family was having, he found out that the one responsible was the mother's sister. He told them, with the mother present. The mother wasn't surprised. She said her sister had always been mean and jealous. At this point in the story, I asked Little Bear, "When you know who is doing all this stuff to people, can't you just finish them off?" It seemed like a logical question.

"I can't do that," Little Bear said, "unless they ask me to." He can know who the culprit is, know what he or she is doing to people, know the individual to be completely evil and unfeeling, and yet he can do nothing about it other than make medicine to protect the person who came to him for help. He can do nothing, that is, until he is asked.

BLOCKING

Little Bear told me about "blocking." He used an example. He had received a call from a man who needed his help. The man had been on his way to Little Bear's house, but his car had stopped running. He never made it. He called Little Bear and told him, and Little Bear started to the man's house, but his car broke down. It happened another time. Little Bear, a mechanic, could find nothing wrong with his car. He figured out that he was being "blocked." Now he can do something to his car to keep that from happening.

BUFFALO

While I was sitting in the living room at the Little Bear house, Sally asked me if I had seen her buffalo. She went to the back room and came out with a piece of luggage and gave it to Little Bear. Little Bear opened it up and pulled out a genuine buffalo headdress, horns and all. Sally handed me a photograph of Little Bear with the thing on his head. He told me that when he had first received it from Joey, the former NFL ballplayer, he had put it on his head, and immediately he had been "sent back." It frightened him. He saw mountains, and he was unsure whether he had been transported to the land the buffalo had come from or to the land of his own, that is, his people's past. It had something to do, he said, with the combination of just what the headdress is and who he is. He has not had it on again, but he told me that he intends to put it on again, sometime when there's no one around to bother him. He wants to see just how far back it will take him. Little Bear told me one time that he believes that we have all been here before. He thinks that God recycles our souls. He's had experiences where he has gone to some place he's never been before, but he recognized it. Who knows? Perhaps the buffalo headdress will help him find out more about this belief.

THE INTERRUPTED SHAPE-SHIFTER

Frank told me about a time when Little Bear took him and his wife to water. Sally went along, too, so there were four of them. They drove to the spot on the creek where they usually go, and there was a man in the creek. Frank said that the man sort of bowed to the four directions. Then he waved his arms around crazily. He danced in the water and ran around, thrashing, mumbling, occasionally hollering. His antics looked absolutely crazy. Frank's wife said, "Goddang drugs." Little Bear laughed. He pointed out an owl on a nearby tree branch, and he said, "That man is trying to change into an owl." They drove on down to another spot on the creek, leaving the man to his antics.

Later when I was visiting with Little Bear, he told me the same story. Here is his version. "It was getting about midnight, so we went off down there. There was this man standing off down there on that rock. He was already into the change, trying to change over. Doing his arms like that. Okay. I had him blocked. He came towards the car, and then he turned. And you know where that little ole dam is over there behind that lumberyard? It was right there on them big old rocks out there. He comes towards the car, and then he takes off. He runs and jumps over to the other side. Then he runs back down into the water and takes off. He runs up on the bank. He comes up across there where the owl's at. He gets over by that owl, and he's wanting to get down. He's wanting to try to change. He knows I'm watching him. He finally gives that up, and he comes across, and he goes back over by his car. I told Sally, 'Let's leave him alone.' He finally got in his vehicle and left. Next day Sally seen him downtown in his station wagon, and he wouldn't even look at her. That was the funniest thing I ever seen. He didn't expect nobody to be down there that time of night, you know." Sally said, "He looked like he was drunk."

SEX IN THE SWEAT LODGE

Frank told me about the woman who used to come to sweats. Anytime she was there, he said, he got an erection. His assistant did, too. He and his assistant talked about it after she was gone. "All she thinks about is sex," Frank said, and that was why it was happening. Frank had to stay inside the lodge until everyone had left and pour cold water on himself. He went to Little Bear and told him what was going on. Little Bear laughed and said the same thing Frank had said. "That's all she thinks about." Frank said that he did not want the woman coming to his sweats anymore.

"GET RID OF HIM"

A woman had a large hump on her back. Someone using bad medicine had put it on her. She was visiting Little Bear for help, and he was working with her, bringing it down a little at a time. Then it would come back. They were just pushing back and forth, he said. This went on for two years. Her sister's husband was doing it. She told Little Bear finally, "Get rid of him." At last the old medicine man who had been doing this to her died. Then his father, also a medicine man, started in, and he was even stronger. Little Bear wound up in the hospital, but he had already doctored her and her house. Some dark shadow was coming in the woman's house. Little Bear said, "Whenever you see it come in, call me." The fourth time she called, Little Bear was in the hospital. He fought to get out. When he got home, about midnight, he felt the thing get in her house. Little Bear was weak, but he fought with the thing anyway, changing shape and tracking it down. Even in his weakened condition, he carried on against it for some time, chasing it, fighting it. Later, he got a phone call from the woman. She said, "Guess what?" Little Bear said, "What?" She said, "That old man died in his front yard."

The woman went in a sweat with Frank, and Frank said that he could smell the old man in there. When they were done, he had to get Little Bear to purify him again. The hump on the woman's back is much smaller, and she is feeling much better, but Little Bear is still working with her. He said that she is doing much better, getting out and going around on her own.

"HE TAKES CARE OF ME"

Many people are hesitant to talk much about what they have been through and what Little Bear has done for them. One young man I met said that he had started seeing Little Bear's grandmother, and when she had passed away, he went to Little Bear. He said that Little Bear had helped him with his ex-wife and then had helped him get his girlfriend back. "Little by little," he said, "she's coming back." He said that any kind of problem he had, he comes to Little Bear. "Sometimes playing softball," he said, "my legs get cramped, and I come to him and he takes care of me." He paused for a long time. Then he said, "I always come to him, and he tells me what to do. He takes care of me." He apologized for not having told me a longer tale. "Mine's probably just basic," he said. "He's always helped me though. Sally, too."

After another long pause, the young man said that he had been raised by his grandparents. After his grandfather died, he had a tough time. He thought about killing himself. He went to see Little Bear's grandmother, and she told him things about himself that no one else knew. Little Bear fixed him up, and, he said, that has a lot to do with why he is still with us.

"I WOULDN'T NEVER GO NO OTHER PLACE"

A black woman came to see Little Bear with her son and his wife. She told me that she had gone to see Little Bear's grandmother some years earlier. Someone was bothering her, and Grandmother gave her something and told her what to do with it, and, she said,

"I had no trouble at all." Grandmother also told her that she was going to have a little girl. The little girl is now twenty-two years old. She helped her a lot with her son. Everything she ever told her worked out. "It was wonderful," the woman said. "I wouldn't go no other place but here." "The first time I came to Little Bear," she said, "I was needing help with my son. It worked out perfect. Everything they ever told me, you know, like one time they was trying to get my apartment, and everything I would do, something would go wrong. I came to see Little Bear, and he gave me some smokes, and the woman never did bother me no more. They've helped me a whole lot. I wouldn't never go no other place."

30

A Typical Saturday Afternoon

I drove up to John Little Bear's house for a Saturday afternoon sweat. It was nearly two o'clock before I got there, and the yard was already filled with parked cars. I found the last possible place to park without going out into the street. There were people sitting in their cars and around the yard. I walked up to the porch. Little Bear was sitting out there, and the porch was full of people. I didn't go inside, but now and then someone would come out or go in, so I knew that people were in there, too. In a short while, four or five kids came running up to the house from somewhere. Frank already had a bunch in a sweat.

Emiliano was there sitting on the porch waiting for his turn at his first round. I sat down beside him to wait. Little Bear was talking with someone about a problem. I soon discovered that there was a large group, six or eight people at least, from the same family. They were having trouble getting along with one another. "Oh, we still pull together on some things," one woman said, "but not like we used to." I wasn't really in on their discussion, but I gathered that their problems had started when their father died. That had been a few years ago. Little Bear asked Sally, "Has it been too long to clean them off from that?" She said that it had not been. Little Bear had them all go through the sweat, and he gave them all medicine to make them throw up, but he had them all also agree to come back together in four days. He'll work with them then when he's not so busy.

In spite of the busyness of the day, Little Bear and I found some time to sit and make small talk. Then Frank came back and said that he was ready for the next batch, which included Emiliano and me. I told Frank that my legs had been going numb on me off and on, and he said that was the stuff coming out of me. He made a gesture when he said it, as if something was going from my head and chest on down through my legs. We all walked on out to the sweat lodge. Three other men went with us. We went out to the sweat lodge and got ready, taking off all our jewelry. I was down to a pair of cutoff jeans and clogs on my feet. Frank went inside the lodge. Frank's assistant shoveled the rocks out of the fire and took them inside. Before making his first trip in, he asked me, "Mr. Conley, do you want it hot today?" Like a fool, I said, "Yes." When he got all the rocks inside, Frank told us to come on in. I went in first. Emiliano followed, and then the others. The assistant stayed outside.

Emiliano and one other man were going through the sweat for the first time, so Frank talked to them first. It was a hot day outside, and it was already terribly hot inside the lodge just from the rocks. Frank told them to relax. He told them if for any reason they couldn't take it, to let him know. "Breathe in through your mouth and out through your nose," he said. Then he poured the medicine on the rocks, and the steam rose. Soon it filled the lodge.

I thought that it was terribly hot, but underneath the incredible heat, I felt cold. I told Frank, but he didn't seem to be much concerned with it, so I decided that I wasn't either. Then all of a sudden, Frank called out to his assistant to open the door. He said that there was something in there that "didn't want to play." Whatever it was, it had come off of one of the two new men. He had his assistant keep the door open for a few minutes, then close it again. I think he poured the medicine one more time after that, and then he went out. We followed. It was a short session, but I felt good coming out, although I staggered a bit at first.

We went back to the porch, and in a few minutes Frank took another bunch to the sweat. Emiliano waited on the porch. He had to go through a second time. Little Bear was back in his room working on some medicine. When he came out again, he talked to a young woman who had a rash on her legs and on the back of her neck. He said that he had read on it, and he couldn't find that anyone had done anything to her. "You're just allergic to the sun," he told her. He gave her something he had mixed up in a small tin, like a Skoal can, and told her to rub it in, and it would clear it all up.

I spotted some friends who had set up their chairs out in the yard, and I went out to visit with them. Pretty soon, one of the women came out on the porch and called everyone to eat. They had spread out some stuff on a table out in the yard. We headed for the table, but the woman called me by name. "Yours is in the house," she said. I went in and found that mine was one of four places set at the table in the kitchen. I ate there with Little Bear and two other people. When I was finished, I got myself a cup of coffee and went back out onto the porch.

In another couple of minutes, Little Bear came back out. We were visiting when Frank came back from the last sweat. He sat down to visit with us, and all of a sudden, he jerked like something had just gotten him in the back. Little Bear had him turn his head and twist his body from the waist to the left. I heard something snap in Frank's back. In a minute or so, Little Bear told him to relax. "It'll be all right," he said. In a few more minutes, Frank went back to the sweat again with yet another bunch. Emiliano went with them for his second round.

Throughout the afternoon, as a car would leave, another car or two would drive up to take its place. One time a car drove up, obviously having problems, and one of Little Bear's sons went out to look at it. His diagnosis: the air conditioner was going out. From time to time, Little Bear sent his son, this same one, out behind the house to fetch some kind of plant, the roots or the leaves or something. Once he sat at the table on the porch dipping a twist of tobacco into warm water and squeezing it. Eventually, he took up a tube made from a piece of cane and blew into the medicine he had made.

Emiliano and the others returned from the sweat, and Emiliano said his good-byes and left, knowing that he had one more day like this to go through. About seven o'clock, I decided that I had better go home, so I said good-bye and thank-you to Little Bear and Sally and left. There were still quite a few people around.

Little Bear was still busy talking with people and making medicine. Frank had at least one more bunch to take through the sweat. It had been a typical Saturday afternoon at the home of John Little Bear.

31

The Stomp Dance

The "stomp dance" is from an age-old tradition in the old Southeast. There are a number of active stomp grounds today in the Cherokee country and in the Creek country in eastern Oklahoma. Each ground has its own ways. They differ from one another in the details of their practice, but at the same time they all have things in common. In the old days, there was an annual cycle of ceremonies that took place on the ceremonial dance ground in each town. Over the years, though, much has changed, much has been simplified. I asked Little Bear and Sally to tell me about the stomp ground today.

First of all, they said, it's roughly like going to church. It's a way of worship, a way of giving thanks to God and praising God for all the good things God has given us. At the particular ground they were describing, they told me, the first dance of the year, the "opening dance," is held in May. It's the time when the squirrels are ready to eat. In late June, overlapping into early July, comes the "arbor dance." During the arbor dance, young women are selected for roles in the coming "green corn dance," which takes place later in July. At the green corn dance, the women dance from 4:00 in the afternoon till 8:00 at night on Friday. After that, they have a regular stomp dance with everyone participating. On Saturday morning, they fix medicine (a drink) and they "scratch." These are both done for purposes of purity. Then the medicine man and the chief of the stomp ground each talk to them and tell them how to behave while they are on the grounds. They tell them not to whip their children and not to leave the grounds without permission. All this time, men have been preparing feathers for the dancing staffs and fasting. At 3:30 in the afternoon, the men dance the "feather dance" till evening. At 11:00 that night, the "regular stomp dance" begins again and lasts until 8:00 the following morning. Then the men dance the feather dance once more.

In August, they dance the "closing dance," sometimes called the "winter dance." At this dance, all of the people camped around the stomp ground go out into the circle to shake hands and tell one another good-bye.

The regular stomp dance is a series of animal dances that lasts all night long. There is a song leader who leads the dancing and the song around the fire in a counterclockwise direction, and there are women known as "shell-shakers" who wear shells tied to the calves of their legs and shake the rhythm as they dance.

Sally told me that in the old days, the locusts told them when it was time for each dance.

32

Spirit War

Medicine men can get to be like old-time gunfighters. Little Bear told me of four Creek medicine men who decided to take him on. They tried to use their medicine to "put him down." Little Bear just used his own medicine to block what they were doing, but each time they would find a way around it. He would block them again. At last they gave it up, and they became friends with him. Today they back him up. If he's busy doing something for someone else, they watch him to make sure that no one is trying to slip up on him. Little Bear has achieved the number one position among medicine people, and as such, he has become a target.

He also has medicine people from other tribes coming to see him, to exchange information about the different ways they do things. He has learned Creek ways, Ponca ways, and the ways of tribes in the Dakotas and in Washington and Oregon. In the old days, he said, Cherokees used medicine when they went to war with another tribe. Now they are using it on one another, "and that's not right. It weakens our medicine when they use it that-away. It ought to be used against the white man that took everything away from us and not on each other."

An old man was chief of a stomp ground, and he had a brother who was a medicine man. But as if the old chief knew something about his brother, he contacted John Little Bear and asked him if he would be the medicine man for this ground. Little Bear asked for a couple of days to think about it. When he had given it due consideration, he went back to the old chief and agreed to serve as medicine man for the ground. The old chief's brother was jealous, but he did not say anything.

Some time later, the old chief knew that he did not have much longer to live on this earth. Again, he contacted Little Bear. "You know that I won't be around much longer," he said. "Who should I pick to take my place?"

Little Bear considered, but not for long. He had already observed the members of the old chief's family. He did not even consider the old chief's brother. He told the old chief that his choice was the medicine man's son, Joe. The old chief nodded his head and smiled in agreement. Joe is kindly, even-tempered, respectful, and polite. He also possessed all the other qualifications necessary for the position. The old chief was pleased to have his nephew selected.

Now Joe's father, the old chief's brother, had not even raised his own children. The old chief had asked Little Bear some years earlier to help him raise the boys. So Little Bear knew Joe like his own son. Little Bear managed to keep things peaceful around the stomp ground for a time, but the old medicine man was now jealous, not only of Little Bear for having been chosen medicine man for the ground but also of his own son, Joe, for being selected chief.

This stomp ground was on land that had been donated to the people. The owner had simply given them permission to use the land. After the third generation of owners, though, there came a change of heart. The young owner had told the people to move their ground. He no longer wanted it on his property. Under the leadership of Joe, the new chief, and Little Bear, the medicine man for the ground, the people moved the ground. The new ground had to be blessed ceremonially. A new fire had to be kindled from the old. But they got the job done.

Then the vengeful jealousy of the old medicine man began to show results. The new ground was threatened. People began leaving the stomp ground. Its very existence seemed to be in question. And all this was because the spiteful old man, jealous of both Little Bear and his own son, wanted it all. He wanted to be chief and medicine man. He wanted the fame and glory for all the work Little Bear had done for the ground. If he could not have it his way, he meant to destroy the ground. And he had the help of a third brother.

Little Bear said none of this would happen. He would not let the jealous old man destroy the ground. He made himself ready for war with the old medicine man, a man ten or twelve years his senior. He rested, he concentrated, he planned his strategy. He said that he knew medicine he had never used, dangerous medicine, but this might be the time to use it. He intended to win this war, and he was fully confident that he would. I was at his house one afternoon when thunder rumbled deep in a clear blue sky. Little Bear was preparing to do battle.

He went to the stomp ground that night and found Joe thoroughly confused, not knowing whether to believe in Little Bear anymore. Little Bear found that three more medicine men had joined forces with the old jealous uncle. Little Bear got Joe away from the others and spent all night doctoring him. Joe began to come to his senses again. Then the bad medicine from the other side hit Little Bear's wife, Sally, and put her in the hospital. They kept her in for a couple of days before she was well enough to go home again. Little Bear's confidence was not shaken. Still he said, "I know I'm going to come out on top. It's just like fighting a war. You got to use strategy."

But one Saturday afternoon, while Frank was conducting a sweat at Little Bear's place, Joe was working as the fire-keeper, and he began throwing logs on the fire disrespectfully. His girlfriend was also in attendance, and he was watching her like a hawk. Later, he was sitting on the porch talking with Little Bear, and he got up and walked away without a word. He told a woman who was there a long story about how his ex-wife was using medicine against him. She had gone so far as to use her own menstrual blood, he said.

Because of the troubles at the stomp ground, Joe asked Little Bear to doctor it. Little Bear had been doing so for years. Still he readily agreed. He went to the ground and doctored it. About a week later, Joe called and said that it hadn't worked. "You must not have done it right," he said. He wanted Little Bear to do it again, so Little Bear swallowed his pride, went back and doctored the ground for a second time. Joe did not call again, but soon afterward, he turned on his girlfriend. They had a joint bank account, and she had put several thousand dollars into it. He withdrew it all, deposited his own paycheck, and put a $200 limit on her withdrawals. He told her, "If you leave me, Little Bear won't do a damn thing for you." Then he went back to his ex-wife.

Joe first came to Little Bear fifteen years earlier, a seemingly hopeless drunk, with no job, no money, and no prospects. Little Bear worked with him and brought him out of it. Joe got a good job and eventually bought a nice house and a good car. Even so, because of the medicine his own father used against him, he has turned on Little Bear and apparently on just about everyone else. The old man wants to be the chief of the stomp ground so badly that he is doing everything he can to cause his own son to lose the respect of those around him. It seems that he is succeeding. Little Bear predicts that Joe will lose his job, his family, his home. He will be "back on the road [drunk] again."

Some more time has passed, and both Little Bear and Sally have suffered heart attacks, and both have recovered. Joe is still messed up, but the old man at the stomp ground, the cause of all the trouble, "can't hardly get around anymore." Still, this story is not over.

A few weeks after writing the above, I was back at Little Bear's house. "Is there any news about the stomp ground?" I asked him. He looked sideways at me with a sly grin on his face and a twinkle in his eyes. "Everything's all straightened out," he said. "That ole medicine man said he was through. He's given it all over. Shut him down. Now he just sits there. Whatever he tries to do just turns back around on him. His eyes are all sunken and black. Whenever I come around, he just sits there. He says hello but that's all. His brother is in the hospital with cancer of the colon."

"How is Joe doing?" I asked.

"He's back to normal. His wife came back to him. Everything's all right."

Joe was back to normal, all right, but he lost his position at the sweat because of his earlier disrespectful behavior.

I was thinking about the old man with the sunken eyes and the brother in the hospital, and as if he had read my mind, Little Bear told me, "Joe's mother gave me the go-ahead. She told me, 'Kill them all if you have to.'"

33

Yet Another One

There seems to be no end to the evil machinations that take place among Indian people and around the home of a medicine man. The writing of this book was unexplainably delayed for several months. It seemed like Little Bear was always busy, and the times I went up to see him, he didn't really have very much more to tell me. We would talk, and I would get a little more information, but not much. Other times he would simply not be available. This seemed to go on endlessly. At last I was talking with Frank one day, and he said, "There's someone who doesn't want this book to be finished." I asked him who it was, but he wouldn't mention a name. Finally, he gave me some hints. "It's someone who's a close relative of Little Bear's," he said. "He's been fighting me for years, because he's jealous of what I do with Little Bear. Now he's trying to destroy Little Bear's medicine." Frank said that he can no longer see the things he used to see. He can no longer pick up the hot stones in the sweat with his bare hands. He's going to have to be doctored over again by Little Bear. "This person is totally evil," he said.

I asked why Little Bear could not combat this evil, and Frank said that when it's in the family, if he fights back, it will destroy the medicine of both people.

"What about those Creek guys who are working with Little Bear?" I asked. "Can't you get with one of them, and . . ."

Frank smiled a little and nodded his head. "That's happening," he said. "That man won't last much longer."

Again, though, I got very little new information from Frank. We talked about a number of things during our visit, only touching now and then on the medicine and the things that were going on with Little Bear. Frank said, "When I look at you, I see a brick wall up about this high." He held a hand up about four feet from the floor. We were both sitting down, so the wall was allowing only my head to show. He said, "Do you notice how we can't talk about this thing? I can't talk about it, and you can't talk about it." I agreed with him. I was supposed to go to Little Bear's house the next day and see what I could get out of him, but something prevented my going.

I did finally did get back with Little Bear, and I sat with him on the front porch. He told me a little bit, but mostly we just sat and visited about a variety of things. I spent four hours at his house, and he was twice interrupted by clients and had to spend some time talking with them and going back to his room to make medicine. I got a small amount of information from the two clients. When at last I said that I should leave and go home, Little Bear said to me, "I had all kinds of stuff to tell you, Mr. Conley, but it just all went out of my head." Time will tell how it all comes out.

A couple of weeks later I went back. This time I went armed with my little portable tape recorder. Little Bear and I were sitting on the porch. One son and one daughter were hanging around, and so we made small talk for some time. At last we found ourselves sitting alone on the porch, and Little Bear looked at me and said, "What do you want to talk about?" I pulled the recorder out of my pocket and turned it on. He said a few words, and I stopped it, rewound it and pushed the play button. It was working fine. I rewound it again and turned it on, and I asked a question. Little Bear started talking, and he told me a pretty good story. I asked another question, and he answered that one. Then I rewound the machine a little bit and started to listen. Something was wrong. I wound it all the way back and turned it on again. It started as before, sounding just fine. All of a sudden, Little Bear's voice turned into a slow growl. I looked at him, and he laughed. I said something like, "I'll just have to rely on my memory." Then Little Bear told me about a time when they had gotten Sally and the kids and Little Bear all together for a picture. They stood together in front of his garage door. When the picture was developed later, Little Bear was not to be seen in it. That happens with him sometimes when technology is being used.

I could believe all of that with no problem. Still, I couldn't help but think that someone was messing with us. Someone did not want this book to be written. I have had people tell me, "Maybe you're not supposed to be writing that book." I can't accept that, because it was Little Bear who told me to do it. I do know, though, that there are people who believe that it should not be done. Whether it is someone like that, or someone who is jealous, or something else altogether, I don't know, but someone seems to be trying to stop it.

34

A Hunting Story

The Indian world is never long without humor, and this real-life story is illustrative of that fact. Little Bear has an older son who no longer lives at home with his parents but comes around occasionally to visit. He was working in Tulsa, and he came home for a visit and to go hunting. James went with him. They were out until the early hours of the morning wandering through the woods not far from Little Bear's home, and they ran out of bullets. "Let's go back to my dad's house," said the son. "I know there's some bullets there." They drove back and went inside the dark house. Everyone was asleep. The son rummaged around with no luck. Finally, he called out to Little Bear, waking him up. Little Bear's booming voice came from the bedroom.

"What do you want?"

"I'm looking for those bullets."

Little Bear rose up with a roar.

"Goddamn you, boy, I'm going to conjure your ass."

"Aw, Dad," said the son, "what you want to do that for?"

35

Dealing with the Legal System

I was visiting with Little Bear one afternoon when a Cherokee family drove up into the driveway. It was a warm afternoon in mid-June. Little Bear knew the people, and it became obvious soon that he had already been working with them. They did not tell me their story, but they talked with Little Bear freely in front of me. The man recognized me from the photo on the dust jacket of one of my novels. He told me the name of the novel he had read, and he said that he had heard stories like that all of his life. His son-in-law had also read the book and was amazed to discover that I wrote it. Little Bear and the man talked about cars and told old stories of their younger and wilder days, laughing and joking. Then with no transition at all, the man said, "They're fixing to file criminal charges on her," nodding toward his daughter. I never did get the whole story, but it had to do with a child. Little Bear asked if it was the child welfare people, and the man said that it was the district attorney. They thought that there was some paperwork messed up or something like that, because they said they just about had everything worked out with the welfare people. Little Bear said that he would read on it in a few minutes. The stories continued for a while, and then Little Bear got up and left us. I continued visiting with the family, mostly the father, who seemed to be in very good humor.

Little Bear came back out in a few minutes and told them that the young woman would not go to jail, that they did have the paperwork messed up, and that everything would work out well. The daughter handed him a pack of cigarettes, which Little Bear unwrapped while he continued the old stories with the father. He opened the pack from the bottom, all the way across, and then he put it to his mouth and breathed into it. Perhaps he sang into it. I couldn't tell. Finally he handed the pack back to the young woman. She thanked him, and her father handed Little Bear some money. They sat and visited with us for a while longer, and then they left. This is not one of the stories that were told to me to be put in this book. I just happened to be sitting there when it transpired.

36

A Night-Goer

A young man's mother phoned Little Bear for help because something was wrong with her son. He was having pains, and he had recently had surgery. Puss was still oozing from the incision. She wanted Little Bear to come to her house, but it was impossible just at that time for him to get away. He recognized what was wrong, though, from the things she described to him on the telephone. He told her to have the young man open up his pocketknife (it had to be his own) and put it under his pillow. He told her what the young man had to say when he did that. The young man did so that night. Sometime in the night, he began to feel the pains, starting at his feet and creeping up his body. The thing was crawling over him and clawing at him. He took out the knife and stabbed at the thing that was causing the pains. The next day an old woman who lived nearby was taken to the hospital for multiple stab wounds to her face. She was treated and released and went right back to work on the young man. Little Bear said that she should have learned her lesson the first time. Now he is going to have to get more serious with her.

37

Three Topics

For reasons that should be obvious, Little Bear is reluctant to talk in much detail about some aspects of his work. These next three topics are good examples. I asked him if it would be all right to talk about these things, and what follows is what I got.

VIETNAM

When Little Bear went into the army and was sent to Vietnam, his grandmother doctored him and gave him medicine to protect him. She took him to a prairie with one lone tree, and they stayed there all day and all night, fasting and dancing around the tree. The tree was for protection. Bullets would not hit him. He told me that he did not get shot in Vietnam. He was injured when someone else stepped on a land mine, and a piece of shrapnel struck him in the hip.

When he came back home after his tour of duty was completed, his grandmother doctored him once again, this time to purify him from the experiences he'd had, to make him forget about the things he had seen. She told him that she could not completely eradicate the memories. He would have flashbacks for the rest of his life, and he told me that he does still have them from time to time. The procedure that his grandmother followed when he came home took four days and four nights to accomplish.

PLANTS

Tobacco is the plant most often used by Little Bear. It can take away pain. For the most common complaints, those caused by bad medicine, he will send his clients out to get a few packs of nonfilter cigarettes, which he will then open up and sing songs into. Mooney calls this "remaking tobacco." Mooney says that the tobacco used is supposed to be the old Cherokee tobacco, but any kind of tobacco can be used if it is "remade." When one smokes, the tobacco smoke carries the message to the spirits up in the sky. Little Bear can prepare tobacco for different uses: for luck, to keep things calm, even to do someone in. Sometimes he will use pipe tobacco, sometimes a twist or a plug. He told me that his grandfather used to plant the old tobacco, the variety used by Cherokees long ago, but when the grandfather died, they could not find his seeds. They must have gone with him. I myself have used Skoal Bandits to cure toothache.

Redroot is used for washing off people who have been in contact with the dead, at a funeral, for example. It is also used in the sweat and to wash someone off after a sweat. It is mixed into water and used as a drink or to wash off with.

Snakeroot can take away pain.

Witch hazel is used to relieve sugar diabetes. It will not cure it, but it will relieve the symptoms. The patient will not have to take pills or shots. A glass a day of the tea made with witch hazel for a month will put a person back to normal. After that, he or she may need to take another glass once a month or so.

A medicine made from a certain cactus will cure diabetes.

Stinkweed brewed into a tea will cure kidney problems.

Cottonwood bark made into a tea for a body wash will relieve swelling.

Yellow root, found in mountainous regions and rocky areas, will cure liver problems. Little Bear says you can tell if a person has liver problems by looking at his or her eyes.

The type of large mushrooms that grow on the side of a tree, prepared properly, will cure cancer.

This is admittedly brief. It leaves out a great deal, but it's all that Little Bear told me.

FEATHERS

Various feathers are used for different purposes. Sometimes the makers of bad medicine will doctor a feather to leave with their victim. When one has such a feather, the only thing to do is to take it to a medicine person who can wash it off. Then it will be harmless. Often when feathers are used in this way, there will be two of them together. Eagle feathers are used for protection, as are owl feathers. The feathers of the redbird, or cardinal, are used in connection with love medicine, or medicine made to help one "catch a woman." A mockingbird's feathers can help someone learn songs. A long time ago, Little Bear said, a man would tie one in his braid while he listened to another singer. A white crane's feather worn in the hat will attract women, but when it is worn by the lead singer at a stomp dance, Little Bear said, you can see it dance. The tip of the feather will spin. On one occasion he fixed up an owl feather for me to hang over the door of my house on the inside. He said that if anyone came "messing" around my house, the feather would begin to spin. A stranger to me, an Indian, had once given me two matching tied feathers. I don't know what they were, but they were black. It was years later when Little Bear examined them. They were a matching pair of bad medicine feathers. Little Bear doctored them to take away the evil that was on them. Then he gave them back to me. They had been rendered harmless.

38

Dillard

Dillard looks like an old white man, but he may be part Indian. Some years ago, he got some medicine books from an old medicine man, and he may have studied with the old man some. He decided that he was ready to use what he had learned, and he had learned shape-shifting. He visited Little Bear's house one night and started "messing with" Alex. Sally knew that something was going on, and so did Little Bear. Little Bear went out behind the house, and when Dillard came out, Little Bear, also transformed by this time, started to chase him. They flew several miles to a place near the university when Dillard turned his head to look back and flew into a transformer on a high-line pole. Sparks and feathers flew, and Dillard landed hard on the ground. Little Bear went home thinking that the fool had learned his lesson.

The next day, Dillard showed up at Little Bear's house holding his hurt arm. Little Bear said, "Those transformers can be pretty dangerous, can't they?" Dillard agreed, but nothing more was said. Soon after that, Dillard and his wife were traveling in Arkansas. There was a work crew mowing along the side of the highway. Dillard's wife was driving, and when she hit some freshly mowed grass, she swerved. The car went off the road and turned over a few times. Dillard's arm was out the window, and when the car came to rest, it crushed his arm. At the hospital, the doctors had to remove the arm. Even after that, Dillard still showed up at Little Bear's house occasionally looking for help. Some people just seem incapable of being embarrassed.

39

It's Not All Medicine

I was sitting on the porch visiting with Little Bear one afternoon
when Sonny called from Oklahoma City. I already knew that his
mother had recently died. Little Bear had gone to the city to be
with the family during the funeral and to doctor everyone who
attended. There had been a huge crowd. Several days had passed
since then, and Sonny had called Little Bear just to talk. He was
worn out from staying with his aging father. Little Bear listened
to him and gave him advice. Sonny has a brother and a sister,
and the sister has grown children. Little Bear advised them to get
together and work out a schedule so that the burden would not
all be on Sonny's shoulders. He advised Sonny that they not talk
about their schedule in front of the old man, as it might make him
feel like he's in the way and cause him to give up. The conversation went on for quite some time. It was not about medicine. It
was about practical advice, and it was about letting Sonny talk
about things that were bothering him. It was about listening.

When Little Bear hung up the phone, though, he told me the rest
of the story. Little Bear and Sally had been to the home in Oklahoma City and doctored it for the mother some years ago. They
had all been good friends. After the funeral, they had gone back to
doctor the home again. When the mother had been alive, she had
followed Sally through the house, closing the doors behind her as
Sally smoked the rooms. This time, Sally went into bedrooms
alone, opening the doors when she went in, but when she came out
the doors "shut themselves." Also, when they got started, Sonny
had turned off the air conditioner. When Sally had finished with
the rooms, the air conditioner came on by itself. The old woman
was still with them.

Her going had been a surprise. She had been to see a doctor who had diagnosed her with cancer. He said that a spot about the size of a thumbnail was showing. Little Bear read on the woman, and he saw the spot, but he saw it moving around. It was not behaving like cancer. In addition, the doctors said that she had stage 4 cancer, but all they were giving her was aspirin. She had a headache, but that was all. Then, when Sonny went to see her, she was sitting up on the bed. She told him that she was being released from the hospital. She seemed in good spirits. Sonny left to get them some food, and when he returned, she had died. Little Bear said that someone had done that to the old woman, and when things settle down a bit, he's going to check it out. Whoever has done this is going to pay.

40

Shape-shifting

with animal

Many of the people who engage in shape-shifting take on the characteristics of whatever animal they take the form of, and they do it only to benefit themselves. Little Bear does it, too, but he does it to go around and check up on people he's looking after. He visits a woman in Oklahoma City several times a week this way.

Little Bear told me that he was taught by several old medicine men. They gathered together in a field, and each one showed him the way he did it. He told me about a medicine man who was parking his pickup in the parking lot of a place where Little Bear's daughter-in-law worked, and he was trying to cause her problems. He wanted to get her fired. Little Bear's son told his father what was going on, and Little Bear told him, "Go see that man and tell him to stop it or else I'll go down to that lot and meet him. He can meet me right there in the parking lot or out in a field, wherever he wants, and we'll just see who has the strongest medicine." The son delivered the message, and the other man did not want to meet Little Bear. He backed off from what he had been doing.

41

The Baboon

Some years ago, Little Bear and his wife and daughter were living in New Mexico. They went to the local zoo one afternoon, and they came across a baboon in a cage. The creature reached out a hand and looked up at Little Bear. Little Bear said that he felt like he understood what the baboon was saying to him. He had some bananas and apples, and he broke up a banana, giving the baboon a piece at a time. Then he cut up an apple and gave the pieces of the apple to the baboon. One of the zookeepers came around and saw him.

"Be careful," the man said. "He's a mean one. He's liable to grab hold of your finger and bite it or something."

Little Bear looked at the baboon and did not see anything mean. He kept feeding it. He was back at the zoo the next weekend and went through the same routine. It became a regular thing with Little Bear and his daughter. Then something happened, and a month went by without a trip to the zoo. When they got back to the zoo, the baboon was not in the cage. Little Bear asked about it and was told that the creature was sick. They couldn't figure out what was wrong. They took Little Bear and the little girl inside where they had the baboon, and it was lying down and looking pretty wretched. Little Bear started breaking up a banana, and the baboon sat up and ate. He had just been missing his regular visits from Little Bear and the little girl.

42

Jim and Steve

Steve called me along about the middle of March. He said his old friend Jim had suffered a stroke and couldn't remember the names of people and places. Jim's daughter had called Steve to tell him about it and to let him know that Jim wanted Steve to drive him to Tahlequah to see "that medicine man." He had to go. I told Steve to come on out. He said it would be about the middle of April.

Steve is a professional photographer who had come to Tahlequah earlier on an assignment. He had been given my name and phone number by a mutual friend, and I had helped him out some. Steve was making his second trip here in order to bring his old friend Jim, a retired chiropractor. He looks, dresses, speaks and acts more like an old cowhand, though. I liked Jim very much right from the beginning. I was sorry to hear about his stroke.

They showed up on Thursday, the fifteenth of April, and came by my house that evening. I called Little Bear. He said to bring them around on Friday about eleven in the morning. I told them, and we sat around and visited some more. Steve told me that he had been misinformed about Jim's condition. Jim said, "I never had a stroke." All they told me was that Jim was having trouble remembering names of people and places.

Friday morning we went to see Little Bear. We found him sitting on the porch. I introduced Little Bear to Jim and Steve and the four of us visited and told jokes for a time. Finally Little Bear started to talk seriously with Jim. Jim told him what he and Steve had told me, that he just couldn't remember the names of people and places. Then Steve broke in. "Tell him the whole story," he said. "He's been going over on the other side."

Jim opened up then. It was something he had done on several occasions—looking for answers, searching for the truth, digging. The last time he had gone too deeply into that place, and when he came back, he had left some of himself behind. Little Bear understood all of this. "We'll have to go back in there and get it," he said. "We can do it. I'll help you."

Done with Jim, Little Bear turned to Steve. "What's your problem?" he said. Steve protested that he was only Jim's driver, but Little Bear asked him again, "What's your problem?" Steve began talking. He had not had a job in five years. He had lost all his enthusiasm for his work. He went on and on. Little Bear said he'd take care of it. He had to read on both Jim and Steve, so he asked me to bring them back at the same time on Saturday, and we left.

We were back at Little Bear's house at one on Saturday. Little Bear had another long talk with Jim. He asked more specific questions about what he'd been looking for, why he had gone over there. Finally Little Bear said that we needed to come back on Monday evening at five. We would be going to water at six. He talked casually for a time with Steve, never again mentioning Steve's trouble.

My wife and I took the two guys out and around on Sunday, trying to keep them entertained. Jim bought two new pairs of boots and a new vest. He was calling us all by the wrong names. We ate out. At last they went back to their motel.

They came around again on Monday. I got them up to Little Bear's house a few minutes before five and again we sat on the porch visiting. Pretty soon Frank drove up. I guessed that Little Bear had asked him up to help. Frank joined us on the porch, and we sat around longer. Finally I heard Frank ask Little Bear how dark he wanted the medicine. "Dark," said Little Bear. "We'll have to let it boil a little longer then," said Frank.

When the medicine was dark enough, Frank poured a coffee can full of it into a bucket of water. He then carried it into Little Bear's back room. Little Bear went in there and sang some songs into the medicine. When they came out again, Frank carried the bucket of medicine into the yard and placed it on the ground. Then he put some chairs around it. A few minutes later, Little

Bear came out of the house with an eagle feather. He and Frank said some things, then Frank left the area. Little Bear dipped some medicine out with a gourd dipper. I couldn't see everything he was doing, but I did see him pour medicine on the ground in a circle. Then he called Jim over and had him sit down. I could see that Little Bear was talking, sometimes to Jim, sometimes as if in prayer. He poured medicine over Jim's head a number of times. He also had Jim rinse his mouth out with it and spit it out on the ground. He kept Jim in that circle for quite a spell.

Finally we loaded up in two vehicles—Little Bear and Frank in Frank's pickup, and I rode with Jim and Steve in their car. We drove perhaps ten miles out on the other side of Tahlequah to a spot beside a creek.

Little Bear said that he and Frank would go to the water and say some things. Then they would take Jim. When they were through with Jim, they would take Steve and me. He told Steve, "We'll take care of your problem." Little Bear and Frank walked to the edge of the water while the rest of us stayed back by the cars. They stood there speaking quietly, then bent over and threw water from the creek over their heads four times, and then washed their feet with water.

They waved Jim over. Again they all stood quietly for a time, Little Bear I am sure was speaking or singing in a low voice. Then Jim squatted down and dipped his hands in the water. Four times he threw water over his head. He washed his face four times. Turning to his left, he walked away from the creek, back over to where Steve and I were waiting. We went next.

We went through the same thing, standing at the edge of the water with Little Bear standing behind us murmuring in a low voice. He told us to throw water over our heads four times and then wash our faces four times. Then he told us to turn to our left and walk away without looking back. It was all done.

He later told us the results would not be immediate, but I could already tell a difference in the attitudes of both men after the end of the ceremony. Jim and Steve left the next morning, in great spirits, headed back home to Virginia and Georgia.

Afterword

This may be one of the most important books I've ever written. I've written more than fifty books, most of them fiction, but I have written a few nonfiction works. None of them has ever given me the problems of this book. Some people have said, and I'm sure many others would agree, that it's because this book should never have been written. I cannot agree with that, however, because it was Little Bear who initiated it.

It moved along well for a while, and then everything seemed to come to a halt. Little Bear would be too busy to talk. Other people would agree to talk with me but would have very little to say. The book was effectively put on hold for months at a time. The publisher's deadline came, and I barely had half the material I had promised. I contacted the publisher and offered to return the advance. They said that they wanted the book badly enough to wait for it.

I tried again to get together with Little Bear but with no luck. I tried to get together with Frank, and he at last agreed to meet with me. He told me there was someone who did not want this book written and was using medicine to prevent it. We talked about everything under the sun but somehow could not get around to talking about anything to do with the book. Then finally I got back together with Little Bear.

He told me to come by his house around 3:00 in the afternoon on a Wednesday. If anyone came around to see him, he said, we'd let Sally take care of them. He said a whole lot had happened since last we talked. I showed up on time. We sat on the porch and talked about a little of everything. Nothing for the book. At last he told me a brief tale that does appear in the book. While I was sitting there, he had to abandon me to visit with a young Creek man for a while. Then a black family came in. Little Bear had to go back to his room to make some medicine, and he told the Creek man and the black woman to talk to me, and I got brief tales from both of them. But the thing that struck me about the afternoon was what Frank had told me already. Little Bear did not seem to be able to talk about the book any more than Frank had been able to. There was definitely something going on.

Obviously, Little Bear was still able to deal effectively with his clients. That was going on more all the time. It was just this book that was stymied. I finally asked Little Bear about it, and he told me that it was true that someone was trying to stop it, but when he told me who it was, it was not the person that Frank had identified. It was someone who is jealous and wants a book written about himself.

A few weeks went by, and I received word that Little Bear had suffered a stroke. I called his house to see how he was doing, and he answered the phone. He said that he was doing just fine. He also said that he had some more to tell me. I went up to the house and found him sitting on the porch. The only visible or otherwise noticeable evidence of the recent stroke was that his mouth had fallen just a bit on the right side. His speech was fine, and he was getting up and walking around. I sat there on the porch with him, but people were calling and coming by, and we did not get a chance to talk for three hours.

At last he told me that he was involved in a major battle with the medicine man who had caused the death of Sonny's mother. The stroke had been a result of that fight. It was ongoing. Little Bear said, "We still gonna win."

Many readers will find the tales told in this book to be fantastic, even outlandish. I can offer no proof of their truth or reality. I have no firsthand knowledge of any of them other than the things that happened to me directly. I can only say that I have talked to a great many people from various walks of life, and the stories that appear here are the stories exactly as they told them to me. I can find no reason to doubt the sincerity of so many different and different kinds of people.

Since I've known Little Bear, he's had a heart attack, pneumonia, and a small stroke. He's recovered from all of them and just keeps working. Nothing stops him. When I went up to visit with him for the last time on this book, while we were sitting on the porch talking, he had five phone calls and a visit from a young white man who had driven up from Ada, Oklahoma, to see him because his wife had left him, and he wanted her back. While the young man was still there, an Indian woman came up to see Little Bear with her own problem. He never turns anyone away. He never puts anyone off. He's like a combination of a psychiatrist, an M.D., and an exorcist, and he's got a lot of Marcus Welby or Doc Adams (from *Gunsmoke*) in him. He helps people whether or not they can pay him.

John Little Bear is one of the most remarkable men I have ever met. He is an impressive man physically, and when one learns more about him, he becomes all the more impressive. He is a powerful man physically and spiritually. He is my doctor, my adviser, and my friend. I can think of no more to say about him than that.

This book has taken me longer to write than any other book I have ever written, and it has not been without its frustrations. Having said that, I will add that it has been a most satisfying experience and one that I would not like to have done without. To the doubters who have bothered to read thus far, I say only doubt on. Your doubts will not worry me, and I'm certain they will not worry Little Bear. His work goes on.

Glossary

ada wehi: A magician.

Agan-uni tsi: Groundhog's mother, from *agana* (groundhog) and *unitsi* (their mother). This was the name of a Shawnee captive of the Cherokees.

Ama-edohi: Water-walker or Water-goer. This name was horribly misspelled by the English as "Moytoy."

Ani-Kituwagi: People from Keetoowah. *Ani* is a plural prefix. Keetoowah is the name of an ancient town. *Gi* is a suffix denoting place.

Ani-yunwiya: The Real (Original or Principal) People. *Ani* is a plural prefix. *Yunwi* is man. *Ya* is an intensive that gets translated various ways.

Asga ya Gi gagei: Literally, "Man Red," the Red Man is a Cherokee personification of the powerful spirit, Thunder.

Asi (this is Mooney's spelling, with a diacritical mark over the "a"; alternate spelling is osi): It is sometimes called a hothouse, sometimes winterhouse. It is a small, domelike house built just outside the larger, rectangular summerhouse. Also used for sweats.

Chalakee: Choctaw for Cherokee, it was used in the Mobilian trade jargon and took the form Tsalagi in the Cherokee language. It was anglicized into Cherokee.

Chickamauga Creek: A creek in northern Georgia. When Dragging Canoe's followers relocated there, they became known as the Chickamauga Cherokees. According to Mooney, the name cannot be translated and probably is not Cherokee.

Cullowhee: A town in North Carolina. It comes from Jutaculla-whee, meaning Jutaculla's place. *Whee*, like the *gi* in Ani-Kituwagi, denotes place.

Echota: An ancient Cherokee place name that can no longer be translated.

Galun lati: Above or on high. Now also translated as heaven.

hilahi yu: *Hilahi* is long ago; *yu* is an intensive.

Jutaculla: The same name Mooney calls Tsul kalu; Mooney translates this, "He has them slanting," but he says that "them" in this phrase is generally accepted as meaning "his eyes." The name is translated loosely, therefore, into English as Slanting Eyes.

Jutaculla-whee: *See* Cullowhee.

Kanati: He is lucky in hunting, usually translated "Lucky Hunter." This is the name of the First Man, sometimes also associated with Thunder. He was the husband of Selu, or Corn.

Kanuga: A scratcher, such as used for bleeding in ceremonies. It is also an ancient Cherokee place name.

Keetoowah: The name of the original town of the Cherokee people. It can no longer be translated.

Kuwahi: Mulberry Place. *Kuwa* is mulberry. *Hi*, like *gi* and *whee*, is a locative.

Mobilian: The name of the trade language used in the old Southeast. It was a highly simplified Choctaw language.

Moytoy: *See* Ama-edohi.

Nun yunu wi: Dressed in Stone or Stone Clad; literally, *nunyu*, "rock," and *agwanuwu*, "I am clothed or covered."

salikwa yi: The green snake or bear grass.

Sequoyah: The famous Cherokee said to have invented the Chero-kee syllabary, his name has been variously translated and even said to be not of Cherokee origin. However, it may simply be from *sikwa*, which originally meant opossum but was changed to mean pig, and *ya*, an intensive, therefore possibly meaning the original *sikwa* (opossum). Sikwa ya, Sequoyah.

Stand Watie: A Cherokee who was a brigadier general in the Con-federate army, he was the last Confederate general to surrender. His first name comes from the translation of Degadoa, a popular name meaning two men are standing close together, shortened to Stand; his last name is shortened from Uweti, meaning ancient.

Tahlequah: A city in northeast Oklahoma built by the Cherokee Nation as a capital city in 1842. There are two popular tales about how it was named. The first tells of three men who were sup-posed to meet and select a spot for the capital. Two met and waited, until finally one of them said, "Tahli eliqua," meaning, "Two is enough." The other is only a slight variation of the same thing. Three men were supposed to find a location where three streams came together. They found a beautiful location, but there were only two streams. The ending is the same. Probably neither story is true. Tahlequah seems to be a slightly different Angliciza-tion of the same word, which in Tennessee is called Tellico. It can no longer be translated.

Tsalagi: *See* Chalakee.

Tsiyu-gansini: *Tsiyu* is canoe; *gansini*, he is dragging it.

Tsul kalu: *See* Jutaculla.

Tsunegun yi: Over there where it is white, a place name, the home of Jutaculla; it is now known as Tennessee Bald, in Jackson County, North Carolina.

Uktena, or ukitena: Keen-eyed. A mythical Cherokee monster, like a giant rattlesnake with wings and antlers and a powerful crystal between its eyes.

Ulunsu ti: Transparent. It is the name of the crystal from the *ukitena*.

GLOSSARY

usga se ti yu: Very dangerous or very terrible.

wa di, or wodi: A naturally occurring red pigment.

Wrosetasetoe: The name of an early Cherokee as recorded by the English. It cannot be deciphered.

yu: An interjection, no translation, but it is often used to close a traditional prayer.